Nonbinary Life

TRANSGENDER THEORY

Series Editors: Ciara Cremin and Abraham Weil

Transgender Theory responds to the contingencies of material, social, and political world-making and the shifting terrains of intellectual histories. This series seeks to publish new works which explore transgender theory, broadly understood, engaging identity beyond gender, including class, race, nation, coloniality, ethnicity, language, ability, and sexuality. Transgender theory emerges out of interdisciplinarity, and thus the series engages a number of subjects, methods, and materialist and psychoanalytic perspectives within the critical theory tradition. The editors welcome submissions which traverse boundaries of bodies, identities, nations, and norms and apply, engage, and author theory in new and exciting ways which help us to understand transgender as identity, phenomenon, and method.

Other titles in the series:

What Gender Should Be, Matthew J. Cull
Let's (Not) Talk About (Transgender) Sex, Riki Wilchins
Transgender Theory, Ciara Cremin and Abraham Weil
Trans Philosophy in a Time of Panic, edited by Matthew J. Cull, Katherine Jenkins and Alexis Davin

Nonbinary Life
An Autotheory

MARQUIS BEY

BLOOMSBURY ACADEMIC
LONDON · NEW YORK · OXFORD · NEW DELHI · SYDNEY

BLOOMSBURY ACADEMIC
Bloomsbury Publishing Plc, 50 Bedford Square, London, WC1B 3DP, UK
Bloomsbury Publishing Inc, 1359 Broadway, New York, NY 10018, USA
Bloomsbury Publishing Ireland, 29 Earlsfort Terrace, Dublin 2, D02 AY28, Ireland

BLOOMSBURY, BLOOMSBURY ACADEMIC and the Diana logo are trademarks
of Bloomsbury Publishing Plc

First published in Great Britain 2026

Series design by Stefan Killen Design
Cover image: iStock/ DENIS Starostin

A catalogue record for this book is available from the British Library.

A catalog record for this book is available from the Library of Congress.

ISBN: HB: 978-1-3505-8893-6
PB: 978-1-3505-8894-3
ePDF: 978-1-3505-8895-0
eBook: 978-1-3505-8896-7

Series: Transgender Theory

Typeset by Newgen KnowledgeWorks Pvt. Ltd., Chennai, India
Printed and bound in Great Britain

For product safety related questions contact
productsafety@bloomsbury.com.

To find out more about our authors and books visit www.bloomsbury.com and
sign up for our newsletters.

for Tessa
for Jinx

Perhaps there's something we can gain by giving up a willingness to be included in the project of gender.

—C. Riley Snorton

CONTENTS

AUTHOR'S (LOVE) NOTE

I don't quite know what I want this to be. Why write such a book? Why say all that will be said here? Well, because I must. It is an offering of thoughts I am sometimes afraid to think, yet I wish for you all to hold them with me in hopes that maybe we'll find, in the caress of one another, some sort of peace amid the maelstrom. What is shared here will be at times hard to swallow, hard to feel good about, hard to confidently agree with. It is for me too. But as we caress one another, we know that at least we have this—the caress.

This is also a frustrated, indignant treatise—a sulking manifesto, of sorts—for nonbinariness. There are many things that are thought about nonbinariness, many feelings we have about our own or others' nonbinariness. We get attached to these thoughts and feelings. They organize our world, and we hold them so tightly sometimes. But it might be that we don't have to hold so tightly, or at all; it might be that if we want to love the nonbinary, if we want to swan dive all the way into that cenote, we can't hold at all.

Maybe this is all those things at the same time. I'll let you decide on that. But whatever it is and whatever combination of those things, it is, in the end, honest.

*
**

This is a book—or rather, a haphazard floating through ideas and experiences and commitments—genuinely felt and dangerously committed to. It says the thing, though there have been moments more numerous than feels comfortable when having said the thing led to someone (or, usually, many someones) being upset. Or confused. Or exhausted. (And let it be known that that someone is sometimes the one who is typing these words.) But, you know, whatever. Say the thing anyway.

There are moments, more numerous than we often wish to admit, when gender simply is not enough. And hasn't been enough—now, for a while, ever. Because it has never been enough, always the terribly ill-fitting mis-name for so many other things we would rather live with and as instead. Always accompanied by a shadowy expanse we've often seen only in the darting corners of our eyes, felt only in the whispered tugs on our coattails when we didn't want to do gender, be gender, speak gender, yet again. These are flashes of the moments when we couldn't quite take the leap into the ethereal thing that loved us without needing us to gender, gender, gender. So now, without equivocation, (or, with many equivocations and awkward laughs and unsure timidities), we will love those moments, with apologies for all the moments we were not capacious enough to do this. This is said for you, for me, and for us—which is to say, all those beings we did not permit ourselves to be. Because gender was far too stingy.

And surely there will be those for whom this does not resonate. That is okay; I bid you all the best in your journey to figure things out. You may even despise some of what is written here. For that, as humbly as I can say this, I am neither apologetic nor indignant, because there are many, I believe, who *need* this, who think so much of these thoughts; who have many of these feelings and may very well live, finally, because this has been written.

This book is giving consideration to those who did not play with Barbies or wear mom's heels because they felt like a girl deep down, who did not envy the boys in class because they themselves were boys and wanted to one day grow up to be a man even though the world kept telling them that their trajectory was decidedly not-man. This book is giving consideration to those who didn't quite feel trapped in the wrong body, and for those who even after their angsty teenage phase continued to not believe in labels. How we come to all of this (*gestures to everything*) is not the point—there are alleys and backdoors and tunnels and hatches that we stumble our way into to end up wherever here is. So it's okay, y'all, if you've felt some of these things, none of these things, all of these things. Because this is for those who feel and have felt, think and have thought, that this is not enough. It is for those who *don't call themselves women and know they are not men. For those who look forward to the day when this will shatter the natural order of men and women.*

Which, I believe sometimes, is many more of us than even we think.

Perhaps we indeed are legion.

xoxo

---

*Kate Bornstein

Part I

16 Bars

For over seven years now and counting, I have been teaching inside prisons. I've taught in maximum security men's prisons where you are pat down, wanded, and metal detected, then escorted by two correctional officers (COs) through gate after gate, each of which must close fully before the next opens, after which you walk across a courtyard overlooked by cells in which people presumed men catcall those these presumed men presume to be women, before finally getting to your classroom. And, a women's prison that, on paper, bears a maximum security status, yet you walk up to the front desk, they ask your name, maybe glance at your ID, lean over the desk to look from their perch into your non-clear bag, and send you on your way through the metal detector that has beeped on more than one occasion due to your belt without more than a "You know where you're going?" It is this latter experience with which I begin this, and more precisely the students of this latter experience.

I've taught these students twice now. The first time I taught them, they dazzled me with how their minds work. We established a rapport quickly, easily, effortlessly peeling away the layers of niceties and small talk that often obstruct genuine connection. When you do any kind of work inside a prison, you are told over and over not to share personal information about yourself with the people you'll encounter. I, with my students in this prison, and every prison before this one, refused this advice. My students know what neighborhood I live in, my partner's name, my mother's name, my life's trajectory, my middle name (when I had one, which I no longer do—and they know this too), and the dimensions of the garden fence we built in our backyard to keep the deer out. And they've, in turn, shared things with me.

One of the things they share, again and again, is their capacity to think deeply and make connections quickly. In my first course with them, halfway through, we read bell hooks. She has a short essay titled "Understanding Patriarchy." During the discussion, one marvelously insightful student made a comment after sharing an anecdote. The student's brother could play and run and do all the things he wished. And the student, too, wished to do those things growing up, but was disallowed because "girls can't do that," the parents said. hooks, in "Understanding Patriarchy," mentions the absolute backlash, physically and verbally violent, she received when playing marbles as a child. hooks clung to the marbles she liked best. *When Dad was at work*, she recounts:

> *Our stay-at-home mom was quite content to see us playing marbles together. Yet Dad, looking at our play from a patriarchal perspective, was disturbed by what he saw. His daughter, aggressive and competitive, was a better player than his son. His son was passive; the boy did not really seem to care who won and was willing to give over marbles on demand. Dad decided that this play had to end, that both my brother and I needed to learn a lesson about appropriate gender roles.*

This scene resonated with my student. "You cannot do what your brother is allowed to do," my student was told. You are to stay here on the porch, with mom and grandma, rocking and knitting and staying put. That is the place of girls, of growing women: here, staying put, on the porch. Domesticated, confined to the sphere of the home. But more broadly, circumscribed by the ascription of gender—it is not I, nor you, nor anyone that is keeping us here. It is simply our lot, by virtue of this thing that we are. And you cannot now, nor can you ever, leave this porch.

"My first prison," the student said, "was the front porch."

Gender's carcerality is not only what it does to those caged but also to those who do the caging, the clocking in, the building of infrastructures that fortify cages, judges and juries that deem for how long someone will be caged. All who are deemed *she* must remain still, legs closed, prim, because you "are a girl," yes, but, too, because gender is a thing that cannot not be abided, and all must do it. There is no out of gender. My student has to remain in place, and that place was the front porch, where gender said girls must remain. And that front porch, an architectural manifestation of gender's reign, was very much, without equivocation or hedging, a prison.

This was my first course with these students, an introduction to thinking about race. At the end, after being asked more specifically about what kinds of things I taught on campus, I mentioned queer theory. "We want that class," they said.

I taught them again two summers later: Introduction to Queer Theory.

The circumstances for this class were different; we were different people. They had learned more, as did I. I was in a different place, they had encountered different things. And specific to me, the weekly meetings began only nine days after I traveled back to Philadelphia for my uncle's funeral, my mom's only brother, incarcerated since I was six months gestated. I still can't bring myself to delete the ConnectNetwork GTL app from my phone, the Securepak website from my bookmarks. But I could bring myself to teach and be taught by these students today.

*
**

This time, unlike my first-time teaching there, I needed to be escorted during the—literally, not figuratively—forty-five-second walk from the front to the education building. I arrive, present my gate pass, even though they should have it on file, and declare clearly that there is nothing in my pockets, placing my see-through backpack in view for them to look through. Then, I walk through the metal detector and wait for my escort. Even though there are at least two people also sitting at the front desk doing, well, not much.

The escort comes and makes unnecessary chitchat. And of course, this being the first day and all, asks what I'm going to the education building for. "I'm teaching a summer class. I'm from Northwestern," I say. And they ask, of course, what I will be teaching.

This is a question that is asked mostly, I gather, out of making small talk, assuming its innocence. Long have I been someone who has told friends that, when describing to them my anxiety and how it manifests, the typical question people ask at gatherings—"What do you do?"—isn't so easy for me to answer. Many people can say accountant or that they work at T-Mobile or Sherwin-Williams or that they're a lawyer or whatever. For me to answer such a question honestly, I'd have to say so many things, things that are uniquely charged. Most of the time I just say I'm a professor. I teach literature. Which is mostly, but not completely, a lie. I hide in the fact that, as I tell them, "I read a lot of books." That usually shuts the conversation down.

It is not out of malice or undue cynicism that I am wary when asked such a simple question; it is out of not knowing where you're at when you are asked this question. I don't know if the person, who I just met, who is asking me a question they deem innocuous because they've likely only encountered people whose responses are inevitably innocuous, is a person I can be vulnerable with in this way. I don't know if I open myself up to unwanted commentary or sneers or physical harm. I cannot simply say, unfettered by whatever prospects might result, that I write and teach and study and am implicated in trans and nonbinary studies, abolition, the black radical tradition, and I think constantly about nonnormative genders and sexualities and would really like to end all this gender stuff. I cannot simply say this without knowing, at least a little bit, what work *you* have done up to this point to make my answer one that will be received. And there is a violence in the presumed innocence of the question. We rarely, if ever, truly know what the asker knows going into the question—perhaps they are secretly a trans insurrectionist who is also uncomfortable sharing their thoughts without knowing where I, the asked, am at—but it still makes me wonder if there are no other ways to engage that open something else up. It is hard not to read the question as a foreclosure, a demand expecting a scripted answer that fits their calculus of validly taught courses or valid ways to exist in this world. Or, to simply let me just teach my class without needing to be surveilled, placed. The question, innocent it may seem and feel, can also sometimes feel, especially in this context, like a "Who are you? What is your business here? Do you belong?"

"Oh, I'm just teaching a class on literature," I tell the CO during our jaunt. Quickly, I add more words, hoping to dilute the possibility of follow-up questions. I've taught here before. I hate the long drive. Nice weather today, right? Sometimes I worry that I am doing a disservice to the folks I care about, to my students, to the nebulously and tiredly named community. I should say the class I am actually teaching—queer theory— with my whole chest, but I don't. I hope I can be forgiven for that. Because maybe that is what my nonbinary does: it evades the grammars of attempted legibilizing. To be made to make myself known on demand, to answer when asked, speak when spoken to might not be what my students—in their learning to love queer theory—even expect from me. They might only expect me to be there with them, not caring how I got there, only caring that I arrived safe. They know what I teach. And it far exceeds being capturable in the brevity of a perfunctory chat with a prison guard. The front porch has massive dimensions.

*
* *

We spent the first four weeks getting our bearings. We read some Foucault and Sedgwick, making sure to think specifically about sexuality and its invention. They were shocked, having assumed all their lives that they just were straight, gay, or bi, and that was it. But to ask the questions we spent over an hour on in class shook them. Because really, is it not

> *a rather amazing fact that, of the very many dimensions along which the genital activity of one person can be differentiated from that of another (dimensions that include preference for certain acts, certain zones or sensations, certain physical types, a certain frequency, certain symbolic investments, certain relations of age or power, a certain species, a certain number of participants, etc. etc. etc.), precisely one, the gender of object choice, emerged from the turn of the century, and has remained, as the dimension denoted by the now ubiquitous category of "sexual orientation"?*[*]

Amazing indeed, and from that moment on I saw the glorious loosening of their ties to "being" whatever sexuality they thought themselves to be. This was the beginning of their gradual refusal of ontological grammars demanded by the state's sociality—of the trappings of being a proper subject; of being proper women, in particular. Once revealed that they did not have to be anything at all, that they could rearrange and anarrange their personhood—that the queerness of the course was not a specific sexuality but cozy with a kind of nonbinariness, which is to say *the extended movement of a specific upheaval, an ongoing irruption that anarranges every line,*[†] where each and every line harks back to gender's demands—they leapt.

We read Judith Butler, Monique Wittig—and got into their beef with one another—and we read E. Patrick Johnson, Cathy Cohen. More than mere content about what happened when and with whom, they were invited to think and interrogate. They asked incisive questions, of the readings and of each other. Two of them, E and D, got into it at the beginning of

---

[*]Eve Sedgwick
[†]Fred Moten

the class. As we waited for other students to trickle in, we talked about the readings, the ideas we were being introduced to. This is Week 4, and we are slowly getting into questioning where we locate gender on someone, what mechanisms of power forced those criteria onto us, and even as we try to re- and deprogram ourselves, we are still in process. D, at that point a self-identified AG (aggressive), had expressed a bit of frustration with another incarcerated person at the prison, S, who was a trans woman (S was not a student in our class). D wanted more people to pause when it came to "taking shots" (of testosterone or estrogen), and was suspicious as to the genuineness of those who were, according to D, all of a sudden interested in shifting the texture of their gender via hormonal means. E pushed back and said that it is troubling waters to assume that D can make assumptions about what people feel and believe and think about what they want to do with their bodies. I listened, rapt. I let them go rather than jumping in. The conversation was intense, but to me, generative, honest, deep, good. Other students looked at me—this went on for ten minutes—and as it began to fizzle, I chimed in and expressed that I didn't think they were arguing; I thought it was a good, healthy working-through of questions.

"No, that was an argument," E said. We chuckled.

These are students living in hellish conditions. Prisons are cages that exile people from their spaces of sustenance and care, from other entities that love them. They sequester those deemed unfit or improper to society under the assumption that prisons are good and necessary. Prisons perpetuate violence. These students, my students, are living amid such violence, contending with the harms of carcerality in numerous ways. And yet they show up to class, because it is a three-hour block of time where things don't simply go on as usual with the mundanity of carcerality. That things so often simply "*just go on*" in carceral institutions, that your meals and your time and your desires and pleasures and livelihood are dictated and structured and regulated and policed, *is the catastrophe ... Hell is not something which lies ahead of us, but this life here.* But our classroom where they can examine and live and love and dare to imagine at least for three hours away from the disciplinary gazes and regulation of COs is a small fissure. And *redemption looks to the small fissure in the ongoing catastrophe.*[‡]

Amid the ongoing catastrophe of their living situations, in our classroom we cultivated something Edenic. No, not that. It was not angelic or perfect; it wasn't utopian—though I like utopias—or without failure on all of our parts. It was, maybe, an honest moment of living, figuring things out, experimenting with ourselves and our ideas, not letting the architecture of thought foreclose our daring to ask other kinds of questions. To teach queer theory here is to participate in an ongoing irruption with them, one that is not neat, not clean, and certainly not safe, but which resists the demand to be known, categorized, or foreclosed.

There are times when 400-level advanced study is a cakewalk for them, but the seemingly 100-level foundations prove troublesome. They grasped shockingly quickly gender's construction, its basis uprooted from the natural or biological. But talking about and using correct pronouns is hard with these students, though not in the way you might think. It's not hard because they don't believe they have pronouns, or are obdurate when it comes to broadening the number of pronouns we use. It's hard because they *do* understand these things, and yet have been deprived of access to conversation and knowledges and people who talk about pronouns in a robust way. But the journey toward, and amid, nonbinary life is bumpy. So even after the week I tell them that Riki Wilchins uses "they" pronouns, that I use "they" pronouns, that Judith Butler uses "they" pronouns, they still default to she, he, and she, respectively. They are not being mean, but still I think to myself, did they not listen when I shared these things before? We even talked about how weird it probably feels—like, at the level of the mouth and tongue—to use the they pronoun for a

---

[‡]Walter Benjamin

single person, so let that allow you to be patient with yourself. We talked about how we will mess up, get things wrong, and that this space—queer theory with Dr. Bey (because, out of an unwavering respect, they refuse to just call me Marquis)—is one where it is okay to mess up, but as long as you are trying that is really all we can ask of each other. So, take your own advice, Marquis. Let them mess up and be patient with them. Where else do they have that chance? How long did I—did you, reader—take to get to a place where pronouns, gender, trans, nonbinary, and the plethora of concepts and ways of life and words and assumptions and ideas felt comfortable?

At the level of spoken and written language it is a feat to elude gender. Our linguistic grammars are suffused with gender; it is literally necessary for the formation of so many sentences, so many ways of communicating. What it means to speak is to use gender, to understand gender as constitutive. So how to get around and through this? I could have told them this instead of internally sulking. I could have also said that "correct" pronouns are not the measure of sufficient gender liberation and ethics. Pronouns can be hard for many, yes, and there is import in using them in ways that lessen harm by attending to which ones another wishes to use. But also, pronouns might still ensnare us in the world of gender we don't really want to be in. To the extent that this queer theory class, then, is not simply the well-trodden history of gay and lesbian cultural events but a nonbinary upheaval of gender's violent hold over the ledger of historical happenings, nonbinary life treks toward genderlessness, so perhaps (these kinds of) pronouns are also subject to the suffixal -less too. How gender has taken hold of language so that we cannot think and speak outside of its sinew. It is, yes, *difficult to be gender 'neutral'. It requires a level of skill that even native speakers do not usually have, the use of a lot of passives and workarounds. We are not trained to speak that way*[§] because gender is all over the place. So we

---

[§]Jespa Jacob Smith

need to get creative. I could have told them all of this to help. They need, as do I, patience to get there.

*_**

The class was searching for language, and oftentimes they found it. By Week 6 there emerged a sort of incantation. Sometimes, though, this language can feel not quite precise enough; and still other times the language inflects other discourses that to some might be imperfect. And this was truest when they kept coming back, each week, to wanting simply to "Be myself." So many of them wanted deeply to just be "me," whoever or whatever they envisioned that me to be.

It came up when we were talking about the "pronoun go-round," where facilitators of whatever sort might go around to all the participants in a given space and ask them to share their names and pronouns. This practice has been praised and critiqued by many, I told them, and the shortest version I can give y'all is this: on the one hand, it's praised because it normalizes asking someone's pronouns and not assuming because they look like a certain gender that that will "match" the pronoun they use (what does it even mean for a gender to match a pronoun?). On the other hand, it's critiqued because it could force some people to out themselves as trans or nonbinary or gender nonconforming when they don't want to, so in many ways it's a practice that just sorta spotlights the genderqueers. Not to mention—which I did mention to them—it's not uncommon for whoever is facilitating, or the participants themselves, to completely disregard "nonnormative" or "unexpected" pronouns, so then why the hell did we waste all this time in the first place?

They understood, even having never heard the pronoun go-round term before, and were on board with the critiques. They, according to many of them, just want to be D or T or R or E, not this pronoun, this gender, because sometimes they don't even know what gender they are or feel like, if any.

There are some people out there who would lovingly try to corral these students, my students, and say that this is a practice of privilege, similar to how white folks—our favorite punching bags—have often swept their privilege away by saying "I'm not white, I'm just Bob" or whatever. And I get that you, whoever you are, want to say that, and deeply believe that. But you don't know my students, you didn't share that space with them and listen to the gifts they gave of themselves. How these terms they've been called don't fit, how they desire and try so hard to enact another kind of world; how they are *not* the women they've been forced to measure up to and instead are something far more capacious and grand. They enact a desire to be simply the unfolding assemblage uncapturable by a pronoun, a gender, tired of the violating skins foisted upon them. Their "I'm just me" is the refusal of a label, a nonbinaristic revolt of the imposition of gendered order and coherence. Because yes, *who wants a title? So claustrophobic, when I'd rather just float away in the parenthetical*, being *uninscribed by language.*[1] These students know a thing or three about what cages feel like. They don't want this cage either.

So maybe the class was improperly named. There are overlaps that nonbinary has to queer, in its concatenated relationship with trans, but what these students journeyed through was emergence into nonbinary life. They took seriously the call to refuse the traps of categorization, to live beyond the boundaries that had been policed into them. Their "I'm just me" resounds coalitionally, not individualistically, as a collective, even abolitionist, rejection of the carceral's demand for legibility. The "just" indexical of a burly anonymity of "me," an illegible "me" that is much more about saying what we are is not definable, that we must desert identity, desert recognition, desert visibility. Anonymous, faceless—*Flee visibility. Turn anonymity into an offensive position.*[#]

In rejecting the pronouns, the labels, the tidy narratives of gender and identity that had long been used to discipline them, they enacted a kind of nonbinariness that far exceeded linguistic

---

[1] T Fleischmann
[#] The Invisible Committee

preference or social practice. They found ways to live that are not predefined, not already delimited by the grammars of state and society. In this, there is an intimacy with the systems that have captured them, an intellectuality and intentional sociality begotten by engagement, by thought, by living. This refusal was not a denial of the systemic forces that shaped them—it was intimately tied to their understanding of those systems. They knew that to shed the label "woman," or to inhabit it in a way that felt cracked open and reimagined, was also to confront the violence of being caged, surveilled, and defined. Nonbinary, for them and for me, bubbles a practice of undoing, a way of carving space outside of the frameworks that sought to confine them. It was an insistence that life, their life, could not be sutured into coherence by anyone else's design.

Understood was the carceral logic of a world that insists on clear lines and fixed identities. They understood, intimately, that the same forces that required them to state their names and pronouns on command were the ones that demanded they answer to other titles: inmate, offender, woman. They didn't want any of it. And in that refusal, they imagined something grander. They imagined a life not bound by cages, by labels, by the state's narrow imagination—or the front porch.

This is the week, Week 7, where we read parts of Riki Wilchins' *Read My Lips* and an essay of mine ("All My Friends Are Trans (or Will Be Soon)"). I hate teaching or talking about my own work. I have anxiety in all but official diagnosis (but the history of trans and nonnormative gender has taught me that a thing can exist without verification from the medical industrial complex). I gave a little history of Wilchins, about the Michigan Womyn's Fest, about Camp Trans, about GenderPAC, and Transexual Menace. I talked for too long. They said Wilchins was hilarious, that Wilchins was a straight up G. And they struggled sincerely, took Wilchins seriously. When they, Wilchins, were vulnerable about their experience being outed and made uncomfortable and unsafe in a group for survivors, the students felt empathy, said that was fucked up. Or when Wilchins said in such clear, incisive script *this is not a book about identities, but about a common cultural machinery—one that repudiates, stigmatizes, and marginalizes many kinds of people. It is a book for anyone committed to changing that system*, the students loved that. Many of them have been incarcerated for multiple decades, some of them were getting released before the end of the course, and one of them, terminally ill, might not live long enough to see her final grade for the class (update: she did, and received clemency to spend her last days at home). These are people who have lived, who have struggled, who have felt the weight of joy and abandonment, and they loved that Wilchins was coming from such a generative grit too. To come from this and commit to no longer parceling out respect and ethics and life chances based on the perfect adjudication of me being me in all the proper ways I am supposed to, you being you in all the proper, approved ways you're supposed to, and then measuring such proprieties as a way to determine what we supposedly "deserve" is all, as they would say, a fucking joke. These students know, even if imperfectly at times, that they are not here to divide one another in the prison they found themselves in based on who did what and who has and received what—they all got put there and are kept there by a system, by a discourse and structure that deems them, my students, unfit for life outside. That machinery is what we are here to do something about. Are you down with that?

We loved on Wilchins' writing before moving to my own essay, which I was anxious to discuss. I shared with them my own trajectory through trans studies, how I understood my nonbinariness. I was asked by one student, T, about what I expected the essay and its argument to do. All I shared was that I am not so utopian to think that my understanding of gender abolition or trans or nonbinary would bring about world peace. I know that the project I and others find ourselves committing to is only one aspect, one piece of things—that it is part of a wondrous mutiny of radical tendrils seeking to engender (or *un*gender) another kind of world for us, all of us. So for all of us to merely identify as nonbinary or trans or to respect everyone else's gender might not lead to the credits rolling and a sense of catharsis. All I want to get across, I confessed to T, and all the others listening, is that maybe I will say these things and someone will hear. Someone will now be a little bit closer to knowing that what mom and dad and neighbor and teacher and doctor and cop and clerk and random kid down the street said need not be true about them. Need not be true about anyone. Perhaps someone listening simply assumed that this is just the way things are—I guess I'm just Cis Straight Guy Bill. And if I'm Cis Straight Guy Bill, I guess I need to do what they say Cis Straight Guys named Bill do.

All I wanted in how I was thinking about trans in that essay, and maybe trans *and* nonbinary in this essay, is to let Cis Straight Guy Bill know that you do not need to be Cis or Straight or Guy or Bill. And maybe that will be the first time Cis Straight Guy Bill is told this. Which means now that person can start again and finally, for the first time, discover something new.

After that attempt at an answer, T said, with a straight face: "Okay, professor, then I think I might be half trans." And we all laughed, because we love that. Because that's exactly what I want. Maybe, and I don't doubt this, T *is* half trans now, and that is a beautiful thing, because think how much more T can discover and explore now, what other things are now on the horizon.

*
**

Week 8 and the students' second paper assignment was due. The incarcerated students I've had over this past near-decade have had a tendency to disregard the analysis requested for the writing assignments and lean much more into the personal and anecdotey. So the running joke for this group of students is that the first course I taught them in, before meeting me but after receiving and reading through the syllabus, they thought I would be a hard-ass. The strictness I included in the syllabus—its seeming unwaveringness—read to them as the policies of someone who was no-nonsense. And then I showed up and "You just a big ol' softie sitting crossed-legged on the desk," J said.

This week's papers were to be on a reading from Weeks 5–8, and included in that span of time was my own article. And two students chose to write about it. I, as I told them, would have never had the courage to write my paper on the professor's own article, but here they were, unbothered and fully confident. The analysis, the understanding, the depth they showed in knowing full well what I was getting at—even as I discuss Gilles Deleuze—was a marvel. One student, B, took my thoughts and ran with them. This is a student who is, at the time of writing, trying to become recognized—though I think we both know this is not the goal, not the right word—as nonbinary under the department of "corrections." So I will call them they, which I hope is okay, B. They offered something beautiful, that what we are after, in this recalibration of trans, invites an *incorporeal freedom*. What a stunning phrase, one that seems to have facilitated, to have characterized their pursuit of nonbinariness. B's incorporeal freedom is refracted through their desire to live in a vastly different way. Prisons insist on the body—its discipline, its categorization, its punishment—as one of its primary sites of control. To enact this freedom of and from a body is one of the many nonbinaries that emerged and pervaded that classroom.

B is a student who has been, since we met, pretty unconcerned with trying to fit in and adhere to racialized or gendered templates. A student who, in a sense, has been pursuing incorporeal freedom for years now. It is not about the body, which is always a body that you are said to have and that needs to align with valid bodiness in order to count as properly a body. This is a student who, in order to be free, desires the incorporeal, the no- and non-body. Desires the no- and nonbinary.

*
**

The end, like all class endings, was bittersweet. We've connected over these ten weeks, formed a bond. We've laughed and learned and argued, and we're better for it. I'll miss that, this time especially. But I will not miss the COs, the small talk chitchat with the escorts; I will not miss the three-hour drive there and three-and-a-half-hour drive back (that damn rush hour traffic); I will not miss the over nine hours of my summer day that I don't get to spend at home.

What sucked most was that the final day was a confluence of circumstances that led to over half the class not being able to show up. Someone had a visit that day, A-Block's line didn't get called, a few were sick, one got into a fight and was on lockdown. So the group was small that last day. We talked about what we learned, how we were different. We laughed, as we always do, and remembered how in our second class meeting, one student, I, went to the bathroom during discussion. The discussion surrounded Foucault and Sedgwick—queer theory faves—and the class sort of, with my help, came to a consensus that "queerness" is not solely a property of people who are designated as "gay" or "lesbian"; queerness is, etymologically speaking (this is the part that was my help), strange and oppositional to a norm, so maybe we are all a little queer at times. Student I came back from the bathroom and T, a classmate in their small groups, said that Student I, too, is queer. During open class discussion, she said, "Well, I went to the bathroom and came back to find out I'm queer now." The class erupted in laughter. This student never spoke; she is quiet, reserved, still figuring out a whole bunch of stuff. And in our last class, we recalled this moment—of revelation; of levity—and encountered it with the intellectual archive of Weeks 3–9. It, as they say, hit different. Because now we know Butler and Bettcher and Wilchins and Halberstam and Stryker and Bey. So when we say queer, we know we mean something so much more than what we thought, than what Mama and Grandmama thought.

And this capacity came through in their final papers. For this population of students, I try to keep them on analytic task for the first two essay assignments, but for the last one, I give them free reign to discuss their lives and feelings and anecdotes.

And this time they did not disappoint. They put their hearts into these papers; I am sitting next to the bulging envelope of them right now, as I write this. To read their experiences, their thoughts, is breathtaking. J, who has been queer in numerous senses of the word since her youth, wrote "because whether you heterosexuals want to admit it: the truth is we're all a little queer, aren't we?!!" You tell 'em, J, tell them that they do not get to believe they are *only* heterosexual; they don't get to believe that they don't have queer work to do, that they cannot shift their desires, their ways of inhabiting the world. D—who, only a week prior, I heard rip a CO a new one, telling him "And it's *Mr.* [D's last name] now. Show me some respect"—wrote, "The 'T' [of LGBT] stands for <u>to hell with gender</u> ... they/them was thought to be ungrammatical because it uses a plural for a singular person. But if I know that I move between many genders and no genders, the grammatical error has been fixed." The swiftness with which J and T—and E and E and R and S and R and M and P and C and C and B and S and M and all the rest—catch on, take ideas and new worlds, and run with them, is enough to make you, as a pedagogue, feel obsolete. But my role in that class was not to teach them, imparting knowledge onto them, depositing knowledge into their memory banks. I've read many things, have thought about all the authors we read; I know many of the authors we read personally and told stories about how I know them, told them about queer theory's history. Yes, I shared those things with them, answered questions of confusion (Dr. Bey, what does "priapic" mean? Dr. Bey, what exactly is a "Stonewall"?). But really, all I was there for was to help facilitate the sharing of knowledge between people who had things to say, who felt things, who wondered, who dreamed, who dared to imagine.

And it was an honor.

I know this was not specifically, solely concerned with nonbinary. The class I taught was queer theory, not nonbinary theory. I know this, and I will not, cannot, and do not wish to conflate queer and nonbinary, or queer and trans, or trans and nonbinary. Yet still, there is something that happened in that space with those students that, to me, was not queer, not trans, but nonbinary.

In that space, we came to know that gender was not our friend. Gender was an unwelcomed guest in that space, showing up when we didn't want it and not really giving us a reason to keep it around. And we came to learn that if gender was in our midst, it meant we couldn't freely leave the house, we couldn't walk around comfortable in our underwear like we wanted, couldn't watch our TV shows, couldn't eat our snacks because gender ate the last remnant of the Cheetos we were looking forward to finishing. It wouldn't let us leave the front porch. Gender didn't let us be; gender limited us so, so much. When one lives in a state-sanctioned, institutionalized network of cages, one becomes intimate with the mechanisms that proliferate caging. One sees that the cage is the steel bars, sure, as obvious and damning as that is. But one also sees the patroller, the judge, the laws created by specific people at specific times for specific reasons, the shift from keys to biometric scanners, the advancement of technology to strengthen surveillance and control, the attitudinal shifts, the sly giving of inches in the form of "gender inclusive" housing to avoid oversight about the harms still present. Those subject to this and those privy to this might see more. It does not guarantee anything, surely, but at the very least when discussing the history of queer theory we could say, in this space with these students, that gender is harmful because, for example, it forces you to become a cop. And then we can point outside the door and say "Just like that," and it will resonate in a profoundly particular way. So if on the receiving end of that pointed digit is gender, the goal is not to queer gender or tinker with it, the goal is not to do it differently; the goal is to live and keep on living knowing that you are able to live and keep on living because gender is not there surveilling you, punishing you for getting out of line, dictating when and where and how and with whom you can do things. To me, this is neither queer nor trans—it is nonbinary.

In that space, none of us were "men," most of them were said to be "women," yet we knew that these gendered categorizations said little of us, gave us little knowledge about each other. At times, especially for many of them, it obscured what others could know of them. We learned that the carceral institution was a violent institution, and endemic to carceral institutions is gender—violence is propounded through gender, through demanding gender, through believing in the need for gender—and that violence need not look like gendered assault or misogynistic harm. It is certainly these things, but also *at other times it is the only way life might unfold.*[**] You cannot get certain accommodations or care without designating yourself as the "proper" gender, you cannot be put in certain housing in which you feel safer if you do not have the "proper" gender designated as vulnerable in ways that validate your need for safety. Even when you are, like a few of the students, trying to become recognized by the department of "corrections" as nonbinary, you need to prove it, jump through the legalistic hoops. But we knew, among ourselves, that nonbinary is precisely, exactly a refusal of needing to prove anything about yourself; indeed, there is nothing *to* prove—there is no criteria or metric by which to validate the proof. To prove, which is to say adhere to a standard by which something can be measured as being the thing it says it is, nonbinariness is a terminological contradiction. These students, in that space, are already invited to nonbinary, have always and already been doing life nonbinaristically, because it is, in its non- and un- and never-gendered course, *open to anyone and forced upon no one. It is radically anti-essentialist.*[††]

In that space, queer theory was just the name of the course, a heading under which we were permitted to read certain authors and engage certain ideas. What we were doing in each week, slowly but methodically, was creating, cultivating, practicing nonbinary life.

[**]Eric Stanley

[††]Robin Dembroff

Carrying What Is Not Mine to Carry

Let's open with a story. My partner and I are in bed, around 7:00 a.m. on a Saturday, having already been awake for an hour, as we are early risers. 7:02 a.m. and we finish the millennial practice of staring at our phones, scrolling Instagram and Reddit for a period of time—debates in r/soulslikes about the best FromSoftware boss only a thumb flick away from r/anticapitalism or r/communism101 strategies for showing up to the riot and surviving tear gas—before shifting our focus to the day. We discuss what our schedules look like that day—mine, answering emails and then playing video games, and theirs, crocheting or throwing pots before responding to emails and then playing video games—and the conversation arrives at a backlog of emails I've been putting off. In the position I currently hold, I find myself on the receiving end of a handful of requests and notes from a variety of people that sing the bureaucratic tune of DEI (Diversity, Equity, and Inclusion) and representation and inclusion and the occasional empowerment discourse. As, of course, one can imagine. It's all very boilerplate—forward this flyer, X organization is hosting a workshop for women, etc. etc. It gets tedious and perfunctory, leaving little room for interrupting the regularly scheduled.

There was one email in particular to which I was not looking forward to responding. I don't remember the specific content of the email, which doesn't really matter at this point. What matters is that the email called for that kind of dance you may be familiar with, the kind of statement that assumes so much in its banality: could you amplify the voice of this marginalized person or group; we *need* to make sure we take this person's gender into consideration; how do we still live in a world where people don't think gender is important? And that is where this story begins.

The email in question tested my political commitments, which is maybe more specifically to say tested my lack of commitment. Gender is important this, women that, you know the routine. And sure, I guess it is. I can't say that these things aren't. But I want to.

I blurted out to my partner: *I don't care about gender.* And they, also nonbinary, were a bit shocked. "What do you mean?" they asked. And I repeated myself, knowing how I sounded but powering through with the statement nonetheless. I was all in: *I don't care about gender.* We went back and forth just a bit, in our characteristic way of simply trying to understand, just curiosity and love: can I invite myself into your lifeworld to more generously sit with you in this moment? Still perplexed, they said that if someone came up to them and asked "Does Marquis care about gender?" they'd respond that "Yes, absolutely. Obviously." And how could one expect any other answer? Nevertheless, after taking a moment to think about whether I wanted to hedge, soften the intensity of the statement, I still stuck with it—I don't care about gender. And I still don't.

So as a clarifying response, I did what I am doing now, and told a story. This time a hypothetical one.

*
**

Okay, so I'm at home, right? I began. And I hear this knock at my front door. My first response is, of course, who the hell is at the door? I'm not expecting anyone, it's probably a random Tuesday and I assume everyone else is also in their respective places of dwelling, and I probably have my comfy pants on. So, I really don't feel like getting up. But the immediate second response is to, of course, go to the door. Alas, there is no one there, but there is a package on the ground. It has my name on it, but I did not order this package. I'm not even curious what's inside this package—it is not mine, I do not want or need it, so I look around for the postal worker who dropped it off and no one is in sight. I might call out and ask, "Did somebody leave their package?" to which no one would respond. I close the door and go back to minding my own business, you know, answering emails and playing video games.

But then maybe I want to go on a walk later. I open the door again and there it is, the package. I forgot it was there because it doesn't concern me, so I trip over it on my way out the door. I'm slightly annoyed, perhaps I scrape my knee in the fall. So, I pick it up and bring it with me during my walk; the post office isn't far from me. Now, people are seeing me with this package. They're thinking, "Oh, Marquis has a package, they must be excited to have finally gotten it" (and of course they wouldn't use *they*). Or, they think to themselves that Marquis is the kind of person who orders packages and likes receiving those packages. But again, this package is not mine.

I arrive at the post office, letting them know this package was left at my door. I did not order it and it is not mine. And they say: sorry, can't help you. It has your name on it; no one else has claimed ownership of it, so it's yours. I say I do not want it, and try to leave it on the desk. They say nope, it's yours, take it, maybe you'll like it, maybe put it on your mantle (I don't have a mantle). And in fact, you don't know that it isn't yours (yes, I do). Look, there's your name. I say it's not mine, I'm good, and they say sorry, can't help you.

So now I'm walking back home and decide, I'm just going to leave the package here on the ground. And when I do so, I get back to going on my walk, but some rando comes up behind me and says here, you dropped your package. I tell the rando no thank you, it isn't mine, and the rando insists. I take it, wait for the rando to leave, then drop it again.

Someone watching from their window might then feel that something is fishy, so they call the police about a suspicious package left on the ground. Now the cops come. They say I can't just leave packages outside, it's a safety hazard. It looks suspicious. Then in my mind I hear the airport TSA—flight cops—announcement: "Baggage and personal items should not be left unattended. Any unattended items found will be treated as suspicious." Leaving, or not wanting, this package is suspicious, nefarious. They say I'm irresponsible, that I'm endangering others. And they write me a citation, give me a warning, tell me that if I leave this package again it will be a criminal offense.

So now, again, I'm walking home with this package that is not mine, that I do not want, that everyone keeps insisting is mine, and I can't even give it back. That package, if you couldn't tell by now, is gender.

I share this story with my partner and things click. I think. They laugh, as do I, and I suppose clarity was reached regarding my offhanded quip.

And though quip it was, there is something deeply serious about it. Truly, I do not care about gender, not because it is not important to many—it very clearly is, if the vitriol I've sometimes gotten is any indication—but because I do not wish for it to be. Full stop. Gender is a thing, a series of things, that demand so much of us. And one of those demanded things is that we care about it and think it good, or if not good, here, or if not here, real and always just around the corner. I don't care about gender because it has nothing for me. No, not even sometimes, as others might note, feeling masculine sometimes or feminine other times and wanting the freedom to shuttle between the two whenever the fancy strikes. I don't even want that, for it, to me, still denotes that whatever we might do is already ensnared in being masculine or feminine or, at the very least, legible on such a scale. We still, even if we use pounds or kilograms, step on the scale expecting an accurate reading. I, however, want to be weightless: to float off of the criteria that has a metric of pounds and kilograms, which only make sense in this particular gravitational press. Were gravity to be different, or to not be—as is very much the case elsewhere—we would literally weigh something else, or weigh nothing, because gravity, we ought to know, is not an immutable feature of every universe. Why insist that all that exists are pounds and kilograms—masculine and feminine—when there are those who float forever, weightless and unweighed, who ask, "What even is 'weight'"? I am not, and do not want to be, masculine sometimes and feminine other times; those terms do not make sense to me, do not need to orient me to myself and others, as if there are not galaxies of other ways to think about this gesture, this piece of fabric, this vocal lilt, or this manner of relation. I yearn fiercely to exist in a world *in which acts, gestures, the visual body, the clothed body, the various physical attributes usually associated with gender, express nothing.** So please, do not merely allow yourself, or me, the ability to choose, now, between the two options. And please, do not allow for the choice of more options of the same dish—McDonald's chicken sandwich, and also Wendy's *spicy* chicken sandwich, and also KFC's chicken sandwich, and Popeye's, and all the rest. How many times do I have to tell you I'm vegetarian?

It is a great task to put down that which we have been made to carry, having built up the muscular strength to hold it, the

---

*Judith Butler

muscular memory to place our arms like this to accommodate the exact contours of the parcel. Indeed, it seems like our arms were made exactly for this task, to carry this very thing. We get attached to things in a world that denies us stability. The attachment helps, soothes, yes. But loosening one's grip allows muscles to rest, fatigue to alleviate, tension to dissipate. Do we not know that our arms can carry other things, can flop down to our sides and take a rest, can *push* instead of carry? Or, that we can carry things on our backs, carry greater loads, or carry absolutely nothing at all, lying in the grass daydreaming of floating?

That is the dream of nonbinary life and living.

It is a peculiar thing, to say no to gender. Gender is by and large not viewed as something that you *can* even say no to. It is not up for debate or conversation. But there are still many, like me, like us, who say no to gender. It happens in many ways, has many different effects. But saying no to gender, in whatever way, is what we're after.

It sometimes happens like this: here is this gender that you have been said to be, and that gender, by virtue of it being gender, is good. You are loved by others because of how well you adhere to and perform the tasks of gender—aren't you mommy's good little boy; what a good girl you've been. The love you feel is routed through gender, so *you* begin to love gender, for it has helped accrue all this love. Or, too, perhaps your gender has not always been so loved; those who share your gender—and what does it even mean to "share" a gender with another? Is such a thing ever possible, that the gender I have is the same as, shared with, another?—may have been through hell because of it. And now, in a moment when hell seems to be softening its grip and opening up room to move differently, you hug that gender with the force of a thousand sentinels because you deem it ethically imperative to do so, honoring all those who have gone through tribulatory conditions so that you can live differently. Now, gender must remain, must be loved, as an ethical imperative.

But don't you know? What put us through hell was gender itself. We've been harmed *by gender*. Gender is not where we find safety; gender itself is the harm, not gender's bad instantiations or bad masculinities or perverse or "warped" iterations of it. No, it is gender that does the harm. Because gender, by definition, demands a certain comportment. Move this way, do not move that way; do it like this and not like that; that's not quite right, it's more like this, actually, but good try anyway; you keep messing up, what's wrong with you, I said it's like this, how many times do I have to tell you?

Can we not feel it, do we not know it? That there are so many moments, small as they might be, where it does not work for us? It makes an offhand comment that rubs us the wrong way, but we ignore it because it has, supposedly, been good to us for so long. Because we've forgotten that this is not the first, nor the second, nor the tenth offhand comment. It yelled at us for not following directions or for taking too long to master its commands, assuring us it'd be the last time. You see, I wonder, honestly, if we are sometimes—maybe more than sometimes—wearing this gender like someone holds the hand of a lover with whom we've known it's been over between us for years.

Gender, far from being an innocent, joyous categorization, is keeping us from so, so, so many things. That categorization *isn't how we acknowledge difference but rather its enforcement, difference leveraged to keep things apart that could well be together*,[†] incarcerating—and I mean this—so many parts of us that could have been free. And for what? Because if this is the case, and it seems to be, *gender has always felt like a prison. I think the whole thing should be abolished.*[‡]

Or, it sometimes happens like this: maybe you've been feeling those flutters for something else, growing dissatisfied with gender. You've been wanting to put the package down and walk away from it without giving it a second thought. But they

---

[†] T Fleischmann
[‡] LJ

bring it right back to you. There is a pervasive assumption that gender is universally appealing. Anyone and everyone should want it. Gender is given and given, even when you don't want it. To be fair, we can acknowledge that this thrusting—I use this word intentionally—could be coming from a sincere place that wants to acknowledge the importance and pervasiveness of gender. Preparing us for the "real world" and all that. And maybe they get a little snippy sometimes when we try to disavow gender, but it's only because they have been around long enough to know that there is a *real, material* basis to gender and the ways it oppresses people. *Women* have been oppressed for millennia *because they're women.* We *need* to acknowledge this; we can't just do away with gender or ignore it. That's just burying your head in the sand.

Yet, how many times do we need to respond that this is not the way things are, nor how they must be? Many continue to begin after the fact, assuming that the fact—that is, gender— is simply fact, unmediated, ontologically transparent, the very ground on which we merely stand. But there is more that lies at and before the "fact." "Women" do not, being simply women, experience oppression that is ready-made for the kinds of people called—indeed, not even "called" but who simply *are*— women. You got it backward:

Unmet needs and sufferings do not spring from a social reality of oppression, which has to be posed against what is said and written about women—but that they spring from the ways in which women are positioned, often harshly or stupidly, as "women." This positioning occurs both in language, forms of description, and what gets carried out, so that it is misleading to set up a combat for superiority between the two. Nor, on the other hand, is any complete identification between them assumed.[§]

[§]Denise Riley

The creation of a class of people hailed as women, and the incessant imposition of gender, is doing the harm; oppression happens, it seems, through the construction of gender. For gender is the child, not the "mother," of sexism and transantagonism.

In the end, these are attempts to manage a crisis. Gender needs to be, so when there is the specter of gender not needing to be or not being, there are wild, manic attempts to bring it back. Because who am I without gender, when "I" is defined as a subject, which is defined by having a gender, defined by the vast archive that gender brings forth to substantiate personhood, sequestered in the *he* and the *she*? I am, it feels like, nothing without gender, so I do not question the system that has been here since I can remember; I question *you*, the problem person in the way of my bliss. I start flailing.

This flailing, this *genre flailing*,[1] can torque itself into a tizzy. It throws the whole litany of things it can at you—it reverts to seventh grade science, to common sense, to "old wives' tales," to jokes about the planetary differences between men and women (and it just so happens that one of those planets rhymes with penis!), all as a way to quell or slow the crisis.

*
* *

I have to ask: what, then, becomes of the body when gender is not carried? What becomes of *my* body, of what they say is my body, when I no longer want gender to authorize it, justify it, restrict it?

Sometimes I wonder, truly wonder, because I am still unsure, what folks like me who move through nonbinariness think about the compilation of impositions, desires, feelings, and contours called our bodies. This is a wondering hard for me to linger with, for what has been called my body—and I trust you will slowly forge an understanding of why I am using such roundabout language instead of saying more simply *my* or *the* body—is also subject to the evanescing suspension of fixity

---

[1] Lauren Berlant

invited by the nonbinary. There are, of course, many ways that gender is given to me when I wish not for it to enter the realm of my living, and that giving is usually foisted onto my shoulders, my genitalia, my voice, my gait—all these inflections of the body I am made to have, in this way, this gendered way, without my consent, without variation, with no hope for it to be or mean anything other than the gendered schema believed to be "natural" to it. And I rage against this like the dying of the light.

There are, though, moments when to have what they say is my body feels quite good. The nonconsensual impositions suck for sure, but the sensations I feel when touched or loved, the affects that ripple like pleasant haptic sensoria when I am held without explanation, when recognition does not precede relation are also what comprise this thing that is said to be my body, aren't they? Yet even still, I hesitate. Perhaps what feels good is not the body as such, but when I am permitted to exceed it—when this form becomes more than the designated vessel for gendered meaning. There is little rejoicing in this body, though there is rejoicing in what it has sometimes been put in service of, and what has moved through and on it; the way it lends itself to inscription, to tattoos that summon anime dreamscapes and philosophical invitations rather than the hegemony of pronouns. Never blank, to be sure, never tabula rasa but tabula script, tabula spectra, carrying the echoes of what else might be written in the stead of the sedimented definite article seemingly required to precede "body."

And perhaps others who find themselves also inflecting and enacting and living nonbinariness feel similarly, wanting not to speak too much of their corporeality but feeling it still, feeling pleasurably, lovingly about it at times. There is this tension, you know, of wanting to float off into some kind of incorporeal realm while feeling and having the capacity to feel precisely because of this amalgam they call your body. Maybe it isn't that I reject the body, but that I reject its conscription. Maybe I am not fleeing flesh, but fleeing the rigid semiotics that would make it mean only one thing. And maybe, in moments—brief, flickering, insufficient but true—what I am feeling is not affirmation of the body but a loosening, an unhooking of it from its assigned grammar. Not love for the body, but love through it, in spite of it, beyond it.

And maybe it's from this place—this hesitant, spectral exhaltation of the body, this weightless desire to exceed its conscription—that we can begin to imagine otherwise. That we can start to ask a different kind of question.

What if we just ... didn't? Imagine if we didn't do gender, didn't demand gender of anyone. Really imagine it. The expectations placed on the unborn, before they can even develop thoughts, would dissipate; indeed, the incessant need to proliferate human life via reproduction in that way might dissipate too, alleviating the ravaging of the planetary ecosystem; what we believe is possible and good for ourselves would expand exponentially: it would mean you do not need to dress in this or that way, and you don't need it to be affixed to feeling a specific kind of relation to gender; you do not have to worry about whether how you walk or talk or gesticulate will signify a discrepancy between how others are reading your gender and what signifiers you enact; you can love or not love or fuck or be fucked or have no romantic and sexual yearnings at all without it implying a propriety with respect to the kind of gender you are said to be; you can be nothing or anything at all. You cannot get thrown over a bridge or shot or stabbed because of another's panic over failing to place your gender, your genre, "correctly" after they've flailed. You can live.

"Gender Is Not the Thing"

One ought to think it unwise to assume that the absolute complexity of life can be reduced to a single thing, that all the existential brouhaha characterizing living in this world is not irreducible, uniquely and generatively complex, joyfully multifaceted such that no one thing has the explanatory power to wrap it all up neatly. And yet, there are moments when this happens. When this one thing is used to clean up the beautiful messiness of life, or that one thing is the end all be all. What that thing is changes and depends on a number of other things, of course. But sometimes, even a lot of times, that thing is gender.

Gender becomes a thing that explains why someone moves this way, dresses that way, speaks in a tone we were told belongs to someone called "man" or "woman." Gender becomes a shortcut through complexity, a placeholder for all that we're unwilling to stay with. That gender swoops in, like some kind of semiotic knight ready to slay critiques or curiosities about something being amiss, reveals an obsession with making gender mean everything, mean *for* everything. Anything can garner meaning and sense if we affix it to gender. Its power lies in its ending of the conversation, no more needing to be said or asked. What else is there to talk about?

But there are some who do want to talk more about it, those for whom gender has only raised more questions. And, those for whom gender *is* a question—or even more, those for whom gender has been taken off the form, fallen out of favor, and is no longer required. And at this moment is when trouble starts, or so it goes. If I don't have you fill out this form, the first question of which is two checkboxes: male or female; or if I don't require this bedrock identifier on your passport, your license, your birth certificate, how will I ever possibly know if you're who you say you are or if you're not up to no good? Because there are no other ways to know if you're really Joe Schmo; I can't just ask your name, I need to know if you're *really* a man. There are no other ways to know if the person before me with the exact face of the person on the ID you've presented me is really you, I need to also know what medical practitioners twenty or thirty or fifty years ago designated as the possible trajectory for the genitals of a newborn infant, so just tell me: M or F? That solves *everything*.

A catchall, cure-all, blame-it-all. Gender is the hinge on which too many doors have been made to swing. Women are acting "hysterical"—it's because of gender. Men are rapaciously harassing and harming anyone deemed not a man—it's because of gender. This thing that has literally nothing to do with gender—that's because of gender too. Gender is the thing.

So, what if it wasn't?

*
**

I am nothing without those who have moved through me, and by that I probably mean everyone. But some have left a trace so deep its ruts are now my veins. Two, in particular, in this instance. They were students, or more precisely friends, or even more precisely imaginations briefly given corporeal form on this earth. In that room, small as it was and partially austere, lined with books that hummed next to us, the Chicago cityscape hazy in the distance overlooking our musings.

We met weekly, without fail. It became a ritual. We'd talk ourselves into knots, pause, circle back, interrupt each other mid-sentence not out of rudeness but necessity—urgency. That's how it felt: necessary. Somewhere along the way, a phrase emerged that anchored our thinking, especially when we got stuck, or when it seemed like others got stuck, on our own inherited languages. *Gender is not the thing*. It wasn't a theory, really, not at first. More like an incantation. A small refusal we returned to again and again when things started slipping toward the familiar and we wanted—needed—another way. It wasn't dismissal. It wasn't denial. It was an opening. A way to say: what if gender isn't the center of gravity, isn't the linchpin? What if our hurt, our joy, our desires, our questions aren't always already gendered in the ways we've been taught to think? What if gender is the decoy, the misdirection, the magician's flourish designed to make us miss everything else? *Gender is not the thing* became our reminder that other things matter too—matter more. A reminder that when gender was made to matter, other things could not matter in ways we wished. That phrase was our permission slip to think otherwise. To keep the aperture open. To refuse the rush to meaning. It let us keep thinking when thinking felt most foreclosed.

What many are trying to do is, of course, account for how we all move through the world. We live in *this* world, so it goes, and even if we want this world to be different we must still grapple with it in the ways it permits. Not doing so, especially when it comes to those who are imperiled precisely by this world, is an injustice, a fantasy you are choosing to live in despite and to the detriment of those most at risk. And goodness, what a powerful response this is.

It's easy to get defensive when those who are far away on the other side of the political spectrum bring disagreements to you. So easy, in fact, you often write them off wholesale, chalking their disagreement up to their entrenchment in an obviously wrong political orientation. But when you are asked a genuine, serious, and thought-through question from someone sitting politically next to you, the two of you just moments ago applauding at the same event, things become more difficult. I had a friend—a friend whose mind and spirit I admire dearly still—ask me the question of how I *live* such ideas. How do I live the quotidian of what can be called, in essence, a nonbinary way of life? How do I address a person over there, a person with certain characteristics that will be and have been read in ways that have fundamentally impacted how that person exists in the world? How do I sit with the fact that, as they said, this *rewiring risks conflicting with the prideful defense of identities that are and have been sites of tremendous oppression and consequent advocacy*?[1] Still to this day, I do not fully know.

But what I shared was, as all ideas are, in process, still being turned over and thought through to its end. Yes, I am one of those people who do the thing where instead of saying, "That guy over there" I say "That person over there." It is a way to make gender not have meaning even in the quotidian, even out of convenient shorthand, a way to not have gender enter into the interaction nonconsensually. It is a way, at base, to not assume another's gender. But this does get tricky: in what ways might not saying "That *black woman* over there" obscure things that are ultimately crucial to note? It can be read as a certain type of "colorblindness" or "postracial" or "postgender" fantasy inanely delinked from reality.

Absolutely, I might say first. This makes sense, and pulls at our ethical commitments. I do not want to make more difficult the fight for racialized gender justice, nor do I wish to unduly disrespect people who are quite rightly bringing up their, for example, trans womanhood as a primary vector through which they move through the world and on the basis of which others interact with them. There is nonetheless still a comfort with which I insist on refusing gender even in the quotidian and deeply personal realms. Because it seems to me that it is a false presumption to think that pristinely articulating such and such a person as black and transgender and woman is akin to mitigating violence. On the contrary, racialized genders, among other kinds of categorization, are imposed apparatuses we are not permitted to live and be socially viable without. So in this context, one where race and gender are not freely chosen but nonconsensual requisites for showing up in the world—and importantly, showing up on the world's terms, terms not of your choosing, terms unable to not be chosen—we "choose" racialized gender largely because we are not permitted to choose anything else, for we are not even a "we," an "I," without having chosen it, without having it chosen on our behalf. What seems more far-reaching and liberatory, loving even, is to try our best to not choose this and to call ourselves and others by other names, by no names, by feelings or dreams or hopes. Calling me by the name of gender keeps gender here, leaves no room for other names or no names, and makes gender, without my say, required for social, existential viability. I am not a person without gender. And people without gender do not and cannot exist. Gender continues to be the thing.

And that classification needs to be placed in order to deem anyone or anything *real*. The desire to define and classify the world, making everything exist only in accordance with a particular worldview, is a decidedly colonial gesture. This *profusion of classificatory options actually harks back to the early days of sexology, when doctors like Richard von Krafft-Ebing,* sexologist extraordinaire absolutely obsessed with naming and categorizing sexual pathologies, *produced new, expert knowledge on human sexual and gendered behavior ... Krafft-Ebing's work on gender and sexuality emerged at a time when Europe was engaged in a large-scale imperial orientation toward classification, collection, and expertise. Our current investments in the naming of all specificities of bodily form, gender permutations, and desire emerge from this period.*[*] But also precede this period: this classificatory violence predates modern sexology. Long before Krafft-Ebing's pathologizing pen, colonial regimes imposed binary gender logics onto indigenous worlds, erasing gender multiplicity in favor of hierarchical distinction. Gender in this way was never merely descriptive—it was a civilizational project, a means of sorting the human from the inhuman, the orderly from the deviant. The colonial desire to fix gender was part and parcel of the broader will to domination, mapping bodies to categories in service of

---

[*]Jack Halberstam

empire. To want, want, want to define and classify just so, just right, is not an innocent gesture of merely wanting to respect. It is a gesture of wanting to know, invasively so, and to know on *your* terms, in ways that make sense to *you*, irrespective of another's desires, maybe, to know and be known by something of which we know not.

Violence does not only happen when, say, the black cis woman is harmed on the grounds of misogynoir; violence also inheres in the naming *as* black cis woman, in the imposition to be—and to be unable to be something other than—a black cis woman (if, of course, such a gendered alignment is possible when proximate to blackness). Because, of interest is the cultivation of a world in which violent apparatuses are, by definition of the existence of that world, impossible. And gender, race, sexuality—all these categorizations that exist ahead of us and are *unable to not be chosen*, for social viability is predicated on being oriented within these categorizations— are, in my understanding, regimes that stanch otherwise possibilities for social emergence. The refusal to name on these categorical grounds asks of us to dare to imagine something that is not already trapped within the paltry possibilities given to preserve the very world we have refused. And it is because I cannot assume that we reach justice when all races and genders are respected and anyone can be whatever gender they wish. That's cool, I suppose, but to me that is not far-reaching enough. What I desire is a modality of relation wherein one need not emerge onto the scene of sociality through these vectors, wherein one does not have to exist racially, gendered, and so forth, in order to exist at all. These things ultimately foreclose that which we might have been were it not for having to be this particular racialized or gendered subject.

We might deem this is nonbinary life: life that wants to live in ways not beholden to mandatory enumeration of all the ways we are said to exist on the current ledgers in place. Nonbinary life does not wish to be, and cannot be, accounted for by the rigid lines and accounts on the sheet used to keep track and tabs. And there is immense, otherworldly freedom in this.

There is freedom, a terrifying kind, in having no place, no box that is proper to you. To have no classification the taxonomic limits of which one needs to adhere, no genre demanding you fit. So many of us want to fit in and belong, and I hear that. Yet still others of us wonder about the joys of not fitting, not belonging, not confined to the lens' framing when there is an open field behind the camera still humming with life.

How beautiful it is when those who dream big are not immediately cast as unrealistic pipe dreamers and out of touch with reality. Because the nonbinary knows that gender is not the thing, it can stretch and flex and not be concerned with trying to fit into the thing's classificatory requisites. It has always been a bad student, falling asleep and daydreaming in class, scribbling outside of the lines and onto the desk, asking the teacher "Why?" too many times. Not to be obdurate—no, it's too unassuming for that—but to be curious, to imagine that there are things beyond these walls, galaxies even the teacher hasn't discovered yet, and we're here on earth thinking it's the expanse of the universe.

*
**

Something needs to be said—responded to—about nonbinary life, and that is the question, the accusation, of its lack of stakes and its class privilege. Not the reactionary claim that nonbinariness is fake or dangerous (that's the Right's tired refrain, and frankly not my concern), but a quieter, more insidious dismissal: that it's frivolous, unserious, the indulgence of daydreamers disconnected from real struggle. That anyone can just say they're nonbinary—poof!—and we're all expected to nod in solemn affirmation. Behind this irritation is a particular resentment: that claiming nonbinariness is a bourgeois maneuver, available only to those whose gender has never really been at risk. That if you were living a real life, a hard life—the kind shaped by poverty, by racism, by violence—gender play would be the last thing on your mind. You'd be too busy surviving to indulge in blue hair and pronouns. The accusation is that nonbinariness is transgender-lite, cosplay for the comfortable. And when someone walks into the room looking too cheerful, too whimsical, too unbruised, it feels like they've skipped the line. Like they've cheated their way into marginality without paying the price. Or so the sentiment goes.

Shorthanded, it would go something like this: only privileged white kids who don't have any real skin in the game would say they're nonbinary; you would really only voluntarily try out a position of gender marginality if your gender has never been up for debate in the first place, and if you didn't have other, more pressing and material concerns of survivability. A bit hyperbolic and unnuanced, I'll admit, but there you have it. And surely there is much to say about this.

What, first, are stakes? To ask most folks is to hear something like "Stakes are having something to lose." And that makes sense. If there is nothing to lose, you have no skin in the game, so how, by implication, can I really be sure that you believe this thing if you have nothing on the line for believing it? I need to know that you will believe this and act on this and support this even if or when they come for you—and more importantly, when they come for us. What, in short, are you willing to give up? How much will it cost you? Do I know that you're willing to pay that price? Will your nonbinariness still be important to you—and will *ours* be important to you—when shit starts to go down? Or will you discard it when it becomes too inconvenient?

Part of the frustration subtending this sentiment is a belief that gender is presumed to rest so deep within the core of oneself, such that no one can ever question it ("Your feelings," or in this case, your genders, "are valid" and that's that), that it in fact has no bearing on or relation to the social. Gender, and by implication nonbinary gender—though I would say wholeheartedly that nonbinary is *not "a" gender—references a core selfhood that requires no expression, no embodiment, and no commonality.* Nonbinariness, therefore, *costs very little. All that is required to be nonbinary is to identify as such, and nobody will be attacked, imprisoned, thrown out of their home, or discriminated against merely for identifying as nonbinary.*[†]

And you see it pan out at times, encountering some enbies who seem to just be along for the ride the exact length of time nonbinary is useful or profitable, hopping off the moment it no longer suits them. And how many nonbinary people can you name who have, on the grounds of their nonbinariness, been imprisoned or thrown out of their home or beaten up? Probably not many. All this would make one think that this whole nonbinary thing isn't what it claims it is.

But then, personally, I have to think again. If for some what is truly necessary to give nonbinary genuine transgressive stakes *is transition—a shift in social gender categories, whatever they may be*, as someone like Kadji Amin notes, we have to wonder what transition is and what properly counts as transition. Is it necessarily medical, a corporeal alteration? This, we know, costs an exorbitant amount of money that, especially when it comes to trans people, can prove prohibitive. But that's not new or revelatory information, let alone a "gotcha" moment for this line of thinking. So many who level the critique already know this. But more questions arise: must transition be medical? And does it end when the medical transition ends (if it ever does end): does the stealth trans person, who has undergone the gauntlet of psychological examinations and gender affirmative medical care and HRT (hormone replacement therapy), still hold the gerundic status of transition*ing*? Can it be legal, consisting of name and identification document changes? Can it be sartorial, a change in style or manner of gait or speech or interest? Must one "come out"? To whom, if so, and how often? Why concern ourselves with the optics—making sure, in order to be truly nonbinary, to cater to the gazes of all those who we do not care about or know, who do not know or care about us, ensuring that we announce on cisnormative terms of legibility our nonnormative (non)genders? It is questions

---

[†]Kadji Amin

like these that emerge immediately when positing a proper template for gender nonnormative life, questions that seem to do more harm than good.

I wonder, too, how many of our enby kinfolk would actually say something to the effect of "Yes, I've *always* felt like this"—a gendered core—instead believing much more likely that one's nonbinariness is the result of a concerted and intentional disaffection with gender. None of us, I would wager—and I know—were decidedly born this way, believing the "born this way" narrative to be the essentialist, cisnormative-logic-driven cop out that it is. In this, perhaps we would not say that it costs very little. We get it, sure—there is little we *have* to do to be nonbinary and there is virtually no barrier to entry. *But that's the point.* We came to this because we are tired of the policing inherent to gender itself, so we move to the tune of something that has declined the imperative to police borders and boundaries. *Policing*, whether tethered to armed patrol or gender, *is a process of capitalist order-making*,‡ and as such nonbinariness will not stand for such policing or disciplining, from anyone. We do not wish to measure our own worth in economic terms ("it *costs very little*") nor do we wish to preordain a correct order for organizing ourselves. Here, we want fields, flowers, and vibes; we want it to be free; and we want it to have the courage to try the impossible and unrealistic. Because the possible and realistic has not done much for us anyway.

We are not interested in affixing authenticity and gender transgressive realness to having undergone sufficiently discriminatory situations. One could after all read the refusal to respond to nonbinariness with overt discrimination (though this is not the only discrimination possible) as a *disallowance* of nonbinariness. One's nonbinariness often might not be read as being real or possible; nonbinariness could often times very well be written off as merely not a thing—so enbyphobes have, supposedly, nothing to discriminate against. Or, put another

---

‡Mariame Kaba and Beth Richie

way, perhaps no nonbinary people—though I do question whether the numbers are actually zero—have been evicted or imprisoned because of their nonbinariness. And? The queer kid from the Christian household who happens to not be kicked out onto the streets is no less queer because they have not experienced this thing that so many other queer kids have experienced, so much so that it often defines queer youth. The trans girl who, beginning only yesterday, understands herself as trans is not "less trans" than our trans elders. Why would we want to literally police gender for queer, trans, and nonbinary people? Why would we want to be cops?[2]

It is, to me, a feat of nonbinariness to elude the evaluative rubrics of gender normativity; that it does not register to others as properly a gender affront gives it a different kind of life. Because gender transgression and gender radicality need not look only like the exact extent of the gender normative's violent response. They don't know what to do with you, so they ignore you—or worse, they don't consider you even there. But that absence of recognition? That's where something new can begin. It doesn't have to mean a shouting match in the middle of the street or a raised eyebrow at the grocery store. It can very well look like nothing to the gender normative, precisely because nonbinary has gone so far away from gender making sense to it. The fight they were prepared for—the defenses they were armed with—don't apply here. *Nonbinary people enact and articulate themselves in ways illegible to the gender-sex system.*[§] It's like stepping out of the ring while they're still throwing punches. I never wanted to fight you, so why would you determine my winning or not winning the fight based on how many times I got punched? I'm not even in the ring.

What, then, of class? It is sometimes a practice, one I've seen on more than a handful of occasions, to use a specific demographic as the foundation against which an implied inverse cannot, or can no longer, claim a legitimacy. When it

---

[§]Sandra Goldstein Lehnert

comes to nonbinariness, what I've heard is that black trans women, often historically named and contemporarily implied, are in conditions of houselessness and thus occupy a *real* class position that does the work that nonbinary people only *think* we're doing.

As it goes, many if not most people who are identifying as nonbinary find themselves occupying a certain class status, and that status is decidedly not "low" (read, by implication, as the "right" class status). By virtue of this, the weight of many nonbinary people's gender politics is diminished because, I think the implication is, if shit really went down, if we really had to lay down our lives or jobs or privileges, we would shrink back into gender normativity, being bold only when it preserved our comfort. Nonbinary folks, many of us, so it goes, are, *before* our nonbinariness, bourgeois, and as such, we will not have class solidarity. Or, would have solidarity with the wrong class. When, say, it turns out that boss man doesn't think trans people exist and that back in his day we didn't have pronouns, will you, purported nonbinary person, say nothing or will you risk your job? Because if you were really down for the struggle, the decision would be clear.

I don't want to speculate here on what any given person would or would not do when the time comes to claim a certain identity. That quite easily devolves into a he said, she said, they said. And, it's not really the point. The point is that what seems overlooked is that *gender is a system of class*, and that *another name for the gender class system is patriarchy*[1]—or more precisely, cisnormativity and the gender binary. To claim gender itself, at all, is to adhere to a certain class; indeed, the imposition of gender onto us all is the workings of a ruling class (call them gender capitalists, say) aiming to control desires, actions, and imaginative possibilities of everyone. The existence of this class system, the requirement to play by its rules, the agreement that its existence is of paramount

---

[1] Vikky Storm and Eme Flores

importance, is what maintains the oppression. Nonbinary, then, nopes out of the system.

And what nonbinariness wants is not a genuflection to the plights, and assumed knowledge that follows directly from these plights, of those who are the ever most marginalized. Nonbinary does not look to preserve the class system, seeking only to slot everyone into their proper place, entrenching a clean and precise chain of command but from the ostensible Left. No, no: if gender is a system of class, and if class does the work of oppression (not only by the conditions that characterize a class but by virtue of slotting entities into a class position in the first place), and further still if the name for the apparatus that maintains and propounds this class system is patriarchy or cisnormativity, then nonbinary becomes the name for *engag[ing] in gender abolition [by] abolishing all forms of class. To do away with gender, so too must go capitalism, race, neuronormativity, and the state.*[#] The State is the byzantine yet aimed organization of control, governance, surveillance, and domination. As a machine of control, simultaneously centralizing and dispersing power through deputization, it creates and forces hierarchies as a means of classificatory Order. Its chief function is to *striate the space over which it reigns, to break up and parcel out, to stabilize and order.*[**] What incisively serves this function, in addition to things like racial, class, and sexual categories of identity, is gender. Bathrooms are broken up and parceled out, check boxes on forms stabilize and order, locker rooms and sports and country clubs and cotillions and debutantes and bachelor parties and baby showers and gender reveals order and parcel and fix. Gender is offered, or more accurately forced upon, as a way of *massacring the body as soon as it's born*, indeed before it is born. And such massacring—such gender; gender as such—*is vital for the production of a productive labour force or the*

[#]Vikky Storm and Eme Flores
[**]Gilles Deleuze and Felix Guattari

productive body. Vital for capitalism.[††] Gender, as deployed by the State, functions as a key technology of control and domination. Since it propounds by striating and coding human existence, enforcing surveillance, and quelling what cannot be categorized through the imposition and maintenance and structuralizing of gender, nonbinary life, then, is a practice—not just against gender, but against the State itself. By refusing the codification of gender, nonbinary life undermines the State's power to manage and dominate, gesturing toward new possibilities of ungoverned, unbound existence.

It can also be said, if the incredible chat I had with a comrade of mine, Levi, is instructive, that nonbinariness is a kind of class *consciousness*. Class consciousness does not end at identifying with a class but is an awareness, a dispositional intellectual affect that can lead to a revolution that would abolish capitalism and the class system. This awareness and consciousness is precisely the condition for the abolition of all classes, all genders in this case; as Marx articulates in a not-very-dissimilar context, *The condition for the emancipation of the working class,* that is, of the gender oppressed, of those oppressed by and through gender—which is to say everyone—*is the abolition of all classes*. Class consciousness, as Levi says, asks us to think of it as a *mode of non-prescriptive coalition*. For one to make the case that nonbinariness is a commitment that shirks itself when it rubs up against the specter of a loss of class status cannot tightly hold what nonbinariness might open up as an abolitionist awareness, a class consciousness. Importantly, class consciousness is more than merely being knowledgeable about the purported class that one is or occupies. Such a position is always arbitrary and developed, regulated, and imbued with meaning by a capitalist system, so we are not to end there, venerating a position that supposedly makes us like one another. Class consciousness, in this iteration of its relation to nonbinary, might not be that we *are* all

---

[††]CB and An

nonbinary, identifying with it and possessing similar sartorial styles; for nonbinary to be a kind of class solidarity comes not from this identification with one another *as* nonbinary but from a disaffection from, desire for the vitiation of, and irreverence toward gender that nonbinary, in this arrangement of the world, names. In other words, one need not be or look the same as other enbies, nor feel one's (non)gender in the same way; one need only to move and move and move away from gender as the grounds on which you move toward others.

Thinking about class consciousness in nonbinary commitments, Levi says, *looks to me like the choice to be conscious of something (the carceral logics of binary gender and its imaginaries about our bodies, and our resistances) and then to mobilize that point.* This does not look like any specific thing; it does not care about looks or even ostensible material conditions, as those conditions do not determine what one does and thinks and believes about the origins or futurity or implications of those conditions. Nonbinariness becomes *inherently anti-visual, unclockable, on these grounds, and more about a type of group oriented by attention and the circulation of an idea ... than by genealogical or material membership. This is, of course, not to say that material membership is not important, but that the self-determination/social restraint catch cannot be solved by pivoting back to the facticity of the body.*[‡‡] Levi might have been too kind, because it might actually, at least to me, be to say that material membership is less and less and less important—again, the "material" is not innocent but also implicated in cisnormativity. What binds nonbinary is not how the supposed demographic of nonbinary people capturable on a census looks and identifies but this capacity to be attentive, to orient away from gender and around any and every entity committed to liberating us from violent apparatuses, committed to loving our possibilities more than anything. What indexes this orientation can't be "the body," for it is lodged still in the

---

‡‡Levi C. R. Hord

purported truthfulness and transparency of materiality. And aren't we way too aspirational to settle for this? Nonbinary is nothing if not hopelessly and hopefully romantic, believing and living as if things can be other than this.

What if trans/nonbinary "commitment," Levi ends, *can look like something other than surgery?* There is no specific "look" to nonbinary, no criteria or necessary procedures. This is openly admitted. There is no way to determine that one is seeing a nonbinary person. It is not a gender with parameters and badges and membership. Nonbinary, through its open-field free-for-all politics of gender not being the thing—which is also to say love and relation and imagination being the things—is evasive, cannot be pinned or fixed, and in not being pinned, scatters to whatever places may be out there.

*
**

This isn't always the case, but one does hear in moments of nonbinary's emergence or articulation an immediate critique. Not the kind you would expect from the usual suspects either ("nonbinary isn't real"; "you're either a man or a woman"; and other such trash). It is unclear the aim or purpose of this particular critique; perhaps it comes from an insecurity as to the respondents' position and commitments, or maybe from a well-meaning reining in of nonbinary's purported overwhelming good. The critique is of course that of race.

Nonbinary, it goes, is white. Doomed to be white. Unbearably white. Can't help but be white. Thus, those who approximate it also, unfailingly, approximate whiteness. The radical project of departing from gender's violence and circumscription is deemed not enough, hemmed by its whiteness, the implication then ending with a kind of "it's not all it's cracked up to be."

What is being touted, it seems, is a deep sense of the historical. People of color have long been subject to the disallowance of proper gendered personhood; the deprivation of gender for, say, black or indigenous people has been precisely one of the primary colonial and white supremacist weapons used to entrench racialized violence. We can think about the ways certain black adults were disallowed femininity, hypermasculinized, infantilized (calling full-grown people "boy," for example), or deemed animalistic; or the denial of "third gender" gender systems, two-spirit people, or the absolute erasure and violent eradication of other kinds of gender cosmologies by European settlers. For these reasons, when nonbinary is cast as a *voluntary* not caring about gender, it rings as sopping with the privilege of never having had to care about gender's contemporary and historical weaponization against you—the privilege of not being racialized in ways where gender was not a given.

It is hard to maintain this critique, though, for at first blush it is reminiscent of a logic that assumes two things: first, that by virtue of one's whiteness they have never had gender disallowed them or, alternatively, that gender, having always supposedly been a given, is not a source of violence. And second, that it is ethical and considerate of the plight of racialized people to *hold on* to gender, that because others haven't had the "luxury" of gender being an overwhelming good that inserts one into the plane of humanity, those who have are ethically bound to keeping and holding and never, ever dispensing with gender. And surely, *surely* we are not about to say this, are we?[3]

We can be generous and assume that those introducing the question of race want to make sure that we attend to differences. We must attend, it goes, to how certain populations have historically and contemporarily differing relationships to gender, such that refusing or claiming gender is borne differently. This is fair, but it is sometimes hard not to feel the whisper of what sometimes is the aim of such a comment: namely, making stark distinctions between how "black people" refuse gender and how "white people" refuse gender. That becomes too taxonomic, and at times makes affordances and differing criteria where we ultimately don't wish them to be. Rather than trying to cleave off appropriate levels of gender or its remaining consideration in mitigated, supposedly ethical forms—doling out gender like rationed bread, careful to make sure everyone gets just enough to be okay but not so much as to be indulgent—nonbinary life, in its inherent entanglement with racialization, insists on a refusal that is capacious *because* of difference, not in spite of it. That is, nonbinary does not overlook or bypass race; it is a praxis that necessarily emerges through the multiplicity of gender's entwinement with racialized logics. It cannot be separated from how gender was apportioned as a technique of colonization, of racial subjugation, of capitalist sorting.

Nonbinary life sits with and beside others who too have been misread, misnamed, misgendered in ways that never felt like simple misidentification but like the orchestrated violence of state-sanctioned legibility. Nonbinary, then, in its most honest and accountable form, can only be committed to a political and ethical life that understands that the refusal of gender is always also a refusal of the colonial logics that produced it as universal.

Like, is it not a bit strange to associate nonbinary—a concerted effort to refuse gender's violence, an acknowledgment that gender has long been neither innocent nor immutable nor universal—with whiteness? The textured and multifaceted departure from gender has a very long lineage of being precisely, too, a departure from whiteness, insofar as whiteness assumes that what is possible is only these two genders done in these very particular ways. It was, after all, not only white European settlers and white supremacists but an obsession with the proliferation of whiteness that instantiated onto non-white populations the gender binary. To depart from gender, we might say, bears indelible traces of insurgent liberatory practices of the black radical tradition and the Global South. Think of how fugitive slaves like Ellen Craft and Harriett Tubman flouted gender while on the run, making *use of gender fungibility*—that is, the ways that blackness collapses gender, that blackness *transes* gender—*as a contrivance for freedom.*[§§] Or how *As Eurocentered, global capitalism was constituted through colonization, gender differentials were introduced where there were none,*[‖] which is to say that a (gender)

[§§]C. Riley Snorton
[‖]María Lugones

binary was imposed where there was no(n) binary. Or how *those defacing assemblages of the flesh,* or those proximate to the blackening effects of racialized violence, *ought to be recognized as putting under erasure the pronouns she and he as well as their attendant gender-sexuated baggage claims.*[##] How on earth can someone say that nonbinary, that the ongoing practice of gender's nonuniversality, its non-immutability, its concerted departure-from, is a white thing?

⁎
⁎⁎

In all of this, an admittedly capacious and free-for-all kind of nonbinaristic thinking, what we don't want is a reductive collapsing. As absolutely rudimentary and basic as this sounds, it bears mentioning that *people are different from each other.*[***] No, not everyone is nonbinary. There are people of various gendered identifications who think of it as natural, as binary, as inherent, as playful, as God-given. And all of these people have varying relationships to gender's use—some weaponize narrow understandings of gender to invalidate others' capacitation of gender, broadening of gender; some use gender to protect them from others' harms. Gender is a sword in some instances, a shield in other instances—but, at the end of the day, remains a weapon.

So no, not everyone lives a nonbinary life. Not everyone is nonbinary. *But the hope is that they will be.*

We need to understand this thing called nonbinary outside of the grammars of identity. Nonbinary cannot be "an" identity, because it might not even be some*thing,* let alone some singular thing one can be. Out of utility and maybe convenience (if we can call it that) we say we are nonbinary, and that carries with it a certain legibility in the current landscape. It doesn't seem like what we mean in the end though; it seems more like a word we use to imply to others that something more is going on. What that more is, is vast and polysemous, such that

---

[##]Alexander Weheliye
[***]Eve Kosofsky Sedgwick

"nonbinary," in the end, doesn't do it justice. But for now, we say nonbinary and call it a day.

We want another grammar for how to live this life. Indexical of that is nonbinary because there is a way it indexes gender's disaffection, how gender is itchy and we want out of that wooly sweater given to us by our problematic grandma; indexical of both a move away from gender but, too and more, a crumbling of gender such that it is no longer a stable, identifiable place away from which to move. Like trans, there are of course many ways to be nonbinary, if we stick with that identificatory grammar. Though this is hardly revelatory or, in the end, even useful. To be honest, I don't really care if there are as many ways to be nonbinary as there are nonbinary people. Cared about and for here is nonbinary's quotidian enactment, its evasive and illegible doing and feeling and thinking. Nonbinary, in its clearest moments, refuses to settle. It can be the glitch in the linguistic matrix when I use roundabout sentences to describe myself or others, never saying "he," as a "boy"; the delay in recognition, pausing for a moment, two moments, three, when I'm he'd by a colleague or acquaintance, a silence even, knowing very well someone is referring to me as "Sir" but not letting the designation land on me. It can be a disaffiliated shrug that doesn't explain itself, like when I am asked again and again—out of respect and care, to be sure—what pronouns I prefer, how I feel about gender. The question can go unanswered, because it is not a question that concerns me. Nonbinary as an atmospheric condition that resists capture not through noise, but through quiet, unyielding indifference.

There are not many ways to be nonbinary. I refuse even this. That suggests a cataloging, a curatorial eye, a gesture toward legitimacy that nonbinary does not ask for. It is the residual trace of a life lived without allegiance to the taxonomical urge. If we turn nonbinary into a thing, *the* thing, we risk making it another node of capture, another site of surveillance and regulation. It cannot become "the third gender" or an alternative box on the census that serves only to expand gender's logistical reach. For some, identifying as nonbinary might feel like freedom—and that freedom matters—but for others, nonbinary might become another structure of expectation, even of exclusion, dictating how to be or not be. What messy residue might be left in this pursuit toward a nonbinary life, as described here, is that it might reproduce the very boundaries it seeks to undo if we don't remain vigilant. So, here's to being vigilant.

But nonbinary's vigilant refusal is not a lone act, not some sovereign individual's opting out. The thing about gender is that it is never just personal, never just mine or yours—it is a structuring force that entangles us in one another's lives, whether we consent to it or not. Those who bear a nonnormative or critical relationship to gender know and concede this, sometimes begrudgingly, present company included. But this does not doom us to doing nothing, never challenging incessantly, never asking questions, never agitating for something else. Gender's wholesale refusal, which is to say, in part, nonbinary life, isn't a retreat into a bubble of individualized self-definition so much as it is a call for a fundamental reshaping of how we relate to one another, how we form and sustain relationships beyond the dictates of gendered expectation. It shifts toward a general antagonism, a collective refusal, a refusal that is not only what I do with myself but how we, together, conspire toward an otherwise—which implicates, at a subjective and personal level, me and what I think about the contours of myself. And this conspiracy cannot be merely a rejection—it must also be a practice of building, of forging relations that do not require gender as their glue but instead make space for the unanticipated, the ungoverned, the unwritten.

*
**

There's a dog walking by: "Look how cute *he* is!"

There's a ghoulish, otherworldly creature in a video game without any ostensible, "identifiable" markers of anything resembling gender: "*He's* so badass-looking."

Dudes and their cars: "*She's* a beauty, isn't *she*?"

Kid finds a cool rock and the parent is like, "Oh, that's cool. What's *his* name?" And kid answers something like, "It's a *girl*, mom! Her name is Rockette" or whatever.

And on and on and on.

Mutants cannot be us. Even droids like C3PO cannot be us. Even dark, scaly alien creatures that are perfect killing machines, that drip acid for blood, come with nasty double-mouths, that burst from the human chest during birth, and drip gobs of gooey saliva before puncturing our skulls are nicely, neatly divided up into boys and girls (the girls lay the eggs, of course).

In short, even our best creative minds are simply unable to imagine, under any circumstances, in any world, in any galaxy, in any alien form, a character who is nonbinary and/or profoundly gender nonconforming ...

This implicitly promotes binary male/female as some sort of unavoidable, universal, and implacable Natural Law, from which [there] is no escape.[†††]

And we know the why, at least in part. Gender is how social interactions happen. Sociality, the quotidian practice of doing the social, is predicated on a dexterous maneuvering through gender and its cues, its assumptions, its violences, its foreclosures. You shake this person's hand in this way if they're this kind of gendered subject; you don't do this with this gendered subject; you can only be alone with this kind of gendered subject (and when you are alone, here's another manual of rules [and if you're alone with the other kind of gendered subject—because there's only one other, of course—that means something *completely* different]); if you are this kind of gendered subject, here's one set of stuff to make sure you buy and wear and maintain and learn to love.

[†††]Riki Willchins

Or, sometimes the social interaction can't even take place until gender is settled, locked and loaded, ready to be deployed. Take, for example, the ever-wonderful, epically queer Judith Butler. They recount a story:

I went into a hotel room in—in London and I was late with grades and I had to connect to the internet and the internet wasn't working and there's a knock at the door. And I'm aware that, you know, grades have to be in at Berkeley at a certain time and, it's like trying, trying, and can't get through and then a guy is there—tall guy. Um, I don't know, I'm short, it matters to me that he was tall. [Audience laughs] And he says, "Excuse me, uh, Mr.—Madam—Mr.—Madam—Mr.—Madam—" Whoa, whoa, whoa. Like, we accelerate and it couldn't stop and so I realized I needed to make an intervention, right, because things were out of control and so I—but I was a little nasty, I'm afraid, and I said, um, I said, "What are you here for?" and he said, "Well, I'm supposed to check the minibar Mr.—Madam—Mr.—Madam." And it starts again and I said, "Is it necessary to determine my gender in order to check the minibar." ... And he left and then later I thought about all the repercussions of this and I thought, you know, he's a worker and ... he was trying to be polite. Gender was, for him, the marker of politeness. He wanted to offer the recognition of gender, so that he wasn't just bluntly asking me a question like, "Can I come in?" like, you know, without addressing me. In other words, he had no way to address me without gender.

There is so much happening here. Most obviously, perhaps, we have the manic oscillation between the only two choices of Mr. and Madam. There are no other choices, yet the person in front of the hotel worker doesn't quite seem to be easily placed into either. So, your circuits are all out of whack now. You blue-screen. This is an interaction that requires gender to be placed, like most interactions, and in not being able to place gender, the mechanisms by which discursive relationality functions are rendered inoperative. Gender must be placed, but gender can't be placed easily. But gender must be placed. But gender can't be placed. But gender …

Now Butler, who is running behind on grades, needs to get things moving. *Is it necessary to determine my gender in order to check the minibar?* That's the question. Because of course the answer is no—the tall person (I won't call this person a "guy")[4] just needs to check the minibar and go on about the evening. Gender has nothing to do with entering the room, checking a thing, and exiting the room. But, also of course, gender *is* necessary to check the minibar: I need to follow protocol, and protocol says there are these genders and based on which gender you are and which gender I am there are specific regulations to follow. Can't determine gender, can't decide which honorific, can't follow protocol, can't move. And we know that Butler knows this, as the capping sentence— *he had no way to address me without gender*—reveals that fundamental to even acknowledging someone's existence is gender. I know that there is a person here whose room I need to enter. To enter, I need permission. But this person's gender is … off. But it can't be off, because to be a person means you have a gender, and that gender is very much, always on. So if there is a person here from whom I need permission to enter the room, that person needs a gender. Now, we're stuck. There is no other way to go about this. Gender *needs to be*.

But what does it say that the imposition of gender (and the impositional is always the intended address, an unasked for givenness or uncircumventable requisite one cannot, normatively, hegemonically, live outside of) is the very road on which sociality treads? What does it say that for the interaction to proceed one *must be* gendered? Accumulative moments reverberate in the womb, with fetuses that haven't even breathed air, sonogrammatically inaugurated, against their will and desire and potential decisions to the contrary years later. To move through the world is to be demanded and required to exist on another's terms, outside the gorgeous maelstrom of one's own modality of subjectivity. A maelstrom that, by virtue of that very maelstrom, undermines the rigidity and linearity—indeed, the discretion and simplicity, purportedly—of a gendered ontology that says M or F. What nonbinariness, thus, queries are the possibilities in not simply correcting misgendering, nor simply being more understanding of gendered difference, but cultivating a form of relationality that undercuts the ontological imperative of gender-as-such *for* relationality.

*
**

As you can imagine, to say some of these things will invite skepticism and indignity, not only from the usual suspects but from those who are generally on our side too. The social justice advocates, the trans and queer kinfolk, the Left-leaning radicals. They, too, will look upon you with perplexity.

There was the person who only in the past month came out as trans, after a lifetime of being harassed and pathologized and harmed for their gender nonconformity. This person looks at me, after listening intently and graciously, points a concerning finger at my face, and says: How dare you? How dare you say that gender doesn't matter (not what I said), that anyone can be trans or nonbinary (is what I said); how dare you try to take this away from me (not what I'm doing, albeit I do want *you* to do that, if by "this" we mean gender)? Or, there was the audience member who, once again listening graciously and intently, recounted in stunningly beautiful detail how excruciating living with gender dysphoria (their words) was and, after beginning HRT and seeing their body shape and distribution shift, is now, for the first time, experiencing gender *eu*phoria. Gender, this audience member said, was their gateway to joy, to love, to accepting themselves.

I can't help, even now, but feel such tearful communion. And, such gratitude for being on the receiving end of this kind of honesty and vulnerability.

That kind of honesty undoes me, still. It tugs at something tender in me, reminds me that gender has, for many, been a way toward survival, toward joy, toward a sense of form where for so long there was only absence. But even this does not quiet my wondering. In these heartfelt anecdotal offerings, gender becomes a deeply personal site of pain or euphoria, where the legitimacy of critique is measured against how well it affirms that personal terrain. I suppose that terrain matters, but it cannot be the horizon. What sits unwell with me is neither their feelings nor their stories of emergence and becoming—I sit uneasily with the way those feelings are asked to become sacred, untouchable, the final word on what gender must be. When gender becomes solely about how it feels to you, it risks becoming untethered from what it does to all of us. I do not want this in the end. That doesn't mean we can't still be moved, still cry together in some kind of recognition. But it does mean we dream toward something that doesn't reify gender. There is room, I am convinced, to dream larger. Some *prefer to make these categories gooey on the inside*, fitting however one wishes to exist, always ensnaring behaviors and feelings. Well, *I prefer to torch them. There's enough room for all at the barbecue*[‡‡‡]— gender need not be at all. And when it is not, then far more fascinating things can come of us.

And I've been witness to it. One moment was particularly powerful. There was a twenty-years-incarcerated black man I had the absolute joy of being able to converse with weekly for ten weeks. We had been slowly working up to thinking about gender in critical ways, but began with more typical, closer to home topics such as blackness and masculinity and growing up in urban, impoverished environments. But then we read about Caster Semenya. I was nervous that this person, among the others who sat with us, would balk at this, make some transphobic or insensitive comment, and try to bring us back to a perceived "real" plight of The Black Man™. But he did no such thing. Without the formal language of cisnormativity or biopolitics he noted that what he experienced, and what he knew others not gendered in the same way experienced, was the invasion of universalizing, white supremacist, cisnormative

---

[‡‡‡]Robin Dembroff

(though he did not have this vocabulary) standards onto people who were deemed outside the norm. What he noticed was that there are eerie similarities between what happened to Semenya and, for example, what happened at Tuskegee. "The same kinds of systems are fucking over me and my brothers, as well as Caster Semenya," he said. In this is coalition. In this is a noticing that rather than trying to jockey over who has it worse, or who adheres more properly to the standards put forth, there is something—gender—fucking us all over. And we, all of us, ain't going out like that.

This is why I find the discourse around authenticity and "real" gender so painfully limiting. Neither us in that room nor those whose lives and knowledges we read about shared an experience of gendered embodiment; what we shared was a critical disposition toward the systems that weaponize it. To center gender as a personal identity project, as something to be named and respected in its specificity alone, is to miss the opportunity for collective refusal. That refusal doesn't always look soft; it doesn't always look affirming. Sometimes it looks like naming the enemy plainly. And sometimes it looks like a person who's been locked in a cage for decades saying, I see how this thing is screwing all of us, and I want out. What might we build if we started from there?

What also happens, and is related to this sentiment of authenticity and policing of proper, real genders (even if those genders are not normative cis genders), is a very particular kind of moment. A moment that, admittedly, has only knowably happened to the one who writes these words on two occasions, but a moment I suspect is largely unsaid though deeply, viscerally felt. It is a kind of moment that exposes that how we are even able to think about what is possible in gendered life is foreclosed by presumptions that define life *as* gendered in a specific way. These moments occur not even in the spaces saturated with hateful, bigoted TERFs (trans-exclusionary radical feminists) but in the spaces of those one assumes will support them: social justice oriented, radical spaces. It happens when you, say, look like me—whatever that look is, and whatever implicit, often unthought-about criteria go into even qualifying as "like"—and are committed to absolutely eviscerating gender. You are *still* shrouded in gender—you are made to, once again, carry what is not yours. Because, you see, one of the things about nonbinariness, if I may, is that I've encountered a few situations in which I—not to mention a plethora of others—am constantly forced back into the normative constraints of this terrain. To understand oneself, myself, through nonbinariness is not to "be" nonbinary; it is to bear, or rather work toward, an unrelation to gender and gender normativity in all its many facets. I have encountered, however, many who tell me that I have "male" privilege. So when I show up to meetings for social justice with the ways my body is shaped and read, despite my nonbinariness and refusal of gender normativity's hold over me, there is a discourse present that demands I not only reckon with but *accept* and reiterate male or masculine privilege as an ethical gesture. They say that someone who looks like I do must acknowledge the reality of how my body accrues benefits bestowed by patriarchy. And if I do not acknowledge this, I wrongly try to rebuke the privileges I undoubtedly, unceasingly, always and forever have.

What these moments reveal—what they demand we sit with, if only for a moment—is how stubbornly gender holds us captive. Even those of us who proclaim to undo it, who refuse its terms and conditions, find ourselves still caught in its jaws. In the ostensibly radical spaces, the spaces for abolitionist praxis or decolonial dreaming, the question of what bodies *mean* remains overdetermined—to be a body that exists, here, now, means that one can only ever be the kind of body said to be possible. And that body is one with gender, with only one of two genders, and each of them have a very specific look. There is something profoundly cruel in this, a cruelty that is neither explicit nor intentional but is, perhaps, the most dangerous because of its unwittingness. This cruelty is the expectation that we must still live within the matrix we seek to obliterate— that I must still live as a man, even as I reject the very premise that "man" is a thing to be lived at all. It is a kind of coercion, a demand that I carry what is not mine to carry, and that I do so with grace and acknowledgment, lest I be deemed ungrateful or unethical. Or just plain out of touch with reality.

And, you know, maybe I *am* out of touch with reality. Reality is doing some sneaky work because what qualifies as real is, it seems, only possible through a cisnormative framework. The real and material and lived conditions are subject to what happens and what other people think and do, how others and systems react to you. We know these others and systems are cisnormative—they believe only that there are men and women, and that privileges accrue in lockstep with those two genders—so for something to happen to me, for me to be interacted with, is to *always* be subject to the whims of the cisnormative. This is then to say that being or enacting nonbinary is impossible, it is by definition unreal, because it rejects the cisnormative, which is real. Put simply: things that are real and that matter are how structures and people interact with you. Those structures and people believe in the gender binary and thus interact with and think about you accordingly. This means they will interact with you and think about you as either a man or a woman. Since these people and structures are interacting with you in alignment with the gender binary, with cisnormativity, that is what is real. Cisnormativity, then, is what is real. Nonbinary is not real, because "no one" treats you not like a man.

How sad this is to think about, that our allies and coconspirators are also ensnared by the seductions of cisnormative logic as logic proper.

In these moments, the limits of radical imagination make themselves known. There is a way in which the gestures to check privilege foreclose the radical possibilities that nonbinariness seeks to open. Because what is the implication here? That I must account for maleness, masculinity, manhood, even as I reject these as categories imposed upon me? That I must enter into dialogue with gender as if its hold over my life is natural and inevitable, as if it is a language I must always speak? It is as if nonbinariness itself—a refusal to adhere to the grid of gender, a fugitive longing for its abolition—is simply an intellectual abstraction, a theory to be politely debated, while I am called back, again and again, into the schema it repudiates. And this is what feels most violating: the insistence that the only way to be ethical is to accept the terms of a game I refuse to play. There is an icky violation at work. At once, these sentiments code my shoulders, my face, my gait without my consent and lock it into a singular semiotic schema; make assumptions of the shape and aim and implications of my genitals; forecast in perpetuity what my interactions can and will look like, what they will mean; and conclude that all of that, that cacophony of interactions and desires and affects and relations, can be reduced to a single thing: man. I cannot determine whether its absurdity is more infuriating or saddening.

What strikes me most in these moments is not only the affective violence of being placed—of having my gender authored by others in the name of equity—but also the structural implications of such an act. Nonbinariness here is not misunderstood so much as misappropriated, folded back into the logic of gender itself. Its radical unrelation to gender is treated as a new form of adherence, a new identity that can be cataloged and constrained within the dominant grammar of the world. In other words, I am not allowed to be unrecognizable, ungovernable; I must be made legible, known. And not just legible, but legible *as a man*, for how else could this insistence on "male privilege" work? How else could this gesture toward recognition and responsibility unfold without returning me to the very structures I work to undo?

Now, they try to place me not out of malice or ill will. That part is clear, which allows me to be kinder, more generous. They try to place and emplot, instead, in order to ensure that privileges and lived realities are heeded. You might be nonbinary and all, the undertone goes, but you're still read as a man and therefore—the syllogistic air implying a logical truism the conclusion of which you are not to reject—you have to acknowledge your male privilege. I know, I think, what they mean, and I know the kinds of politics and discourses from which they draw. And those things are generally good, which I appreciate. It seems too often, though, that the requisite to acknowledge and check is in fact a requisite to content myself with the existing order as if it is natural, as if nothing can—or should—be done about it. Where is, I continue to ask, the love of dreaming of other lives we can live? What lack of generosity for the kinds of beings, the kinds of love and lives, the beautiful possibilities we might be introduced to. I want *that*, and now. We have waited too long for those things. And it is curious why even when there is an express desire for the dismantling of this world, there is not only a lack of desire but a decided resistance to dismantling this. What is that about? Why does the imagination stumble when it comes to gender? It is as if the conceptual architecture of this world has rendered gender as an immovable object, a given so fixed that even radical politics seem incapable of approaching it with the same rigor as they do other forms of oppression. Perhaps this is why the affect of these exchanges feels so laden with pessimism: the undertone is not one of curiosity or solidarity but of a begrudging insistence on holding the line.

It seems often that they want me to be a man. And how cruel is that, how violent, to me and others. In a sly undermining of the political valence and intention of nonbinariness (e.g., to subvert, interrogate, and displace the assumption that a body means something *a priori* and that gender can be assumed by making recourse to the corporeal surface), I am called to deem and make myself, over and over, a legible man in a perverse commitment to gendered ethics.

So there is a bracing. 'Cause what I want to say in response to "You have to acknowledge your male privilege" is: *No, I don't.* Because on the one hand, it is not too difficult to recognize the TERF-y rationale here. Many a trans-exclusionary person, feminist-identified or not, notes that, say, trans women are not women because they have been socialized as men, are treated as men by many people, or worse yet have "male energy." Similarly here, one might be nonbinary, but they are still socialized as men and are interacted with by others as men and thus are bestowed, in a word, a "manness" that, I would argue, is assumed more true and important for their purposes of social justice. In short, what they say you are is, then, what you are. You are ultimately not allowed to be nonbinary. On the other hand, when will we allow for the disaggregating of a look from an entire world? There is time and again a whole archive unleashed onto one when they appear to others in a certain way. Those others already have in mind only two ways that one is able to show up, and there is a rigidity to those two ways, so even if there is confusion, not-quite-fits, not-fully-theres, one of the two ways is still placed. And once placed, that dredges up vast worlds the one who is placed is forced to contend with, even though they may not want to, may have long disavowed that world and are living, as desperately as their will to survive will allow, far away somewhere else with more lush existential fields. But the world placed onto them, before and ahead of them, is the only world that is "real."

I don't want it. Don't need it. And will live anyway.

Part II

Burner Gender

These categories are the map imposed by authority, not the territory of life.
—Paul Preciado, *An Apartment on Uranus*

My older brother had a friend maybe two decades ago—he has since been killed—who once came to our house to play NBA 2K-whatever-year. I was but eleven or twelve, and this friend had two phones. First, I thought he was just that rich, enough disposable income for not one but two cellphones. Turns out, according to my brother, one was the phone he used for buying and selling drugs. "That's his burner," my brother said. I only pretended to understand.

Since, the concept has become more clarified. That cheap, plastic shell, then, I imagine, felt both liberating and incriminating. The burner phone materializes when certain kinds of connections need to be made without the dusty debris that our digital tire tracks so eagerly leave behind. It is a device so unassuming, almost innocuous in its simplicity, yet it carries with it the weight of anonymity that even more so now our smartphones, with their biometric locks and cloud backups, can never afford us. The burner phone is stripped almost to its barest: a voice, a number, a time, and location with one objective, untethered from me being Me or you being You, dancing at the edges of legitimacy.

And it seems inextricable from its illicity, its shadowy liminality between safety and secrecy, between freedom and surveillance. The burner phone, at base, is an object of temporary utility, an apparatus meant to dissolve into nothingness as soon as its purpose is fulfilled. It is, in this sense, a performative contradiction: a tool meant to connect, that purports to connect, yet its very existence is predicated on disconnection—disconnection from identity, from traceability, from the networks that it relies on to function and track.

The conceit of the phone is that it definitionally connects those who use it. And yet the burner phone connects on a slant; it connects and then, a week later, or a day later, there is no connection. It is in fact rerouted in service of disconnection, slipping through the cracks of surveillance that have become the default setting of modern existence, yearning for the unmonitored and conversations beyond the algorithms of data and accounting.

In some ways, the burner phone purports, but does not deliver on, its performance of the task it has been made to perform. It performs its role badly.

Much ink has been spilled over understandings of the notion of gender performativity. Even more ink has been spilled over misunderstandings of it, that it is merely a performance. Clarifying the difference, Judith Butler notes, somewhat famously:

JB   *Well, there is a bad reading, which unfortunately is the most popular one. The bad reading goes something like this: I can get up in the morning, look in my closet, and decide which gender I want to be today. I can take out a piece of clothing and change my gender, stylize it, and then that evening I can change it again and be something radically other, so that what you get is something like the commodification of gender, and the understanding of taking on a gender as a kind of consumerism.*

LK   [Liz Kotz, *the interviewer*] *And also as a totally*
          volitional act …

JB   *… . on the part of a subject who treats gender quite*
          deliberately, as if it's an object out there, when my
          whole point was that the very formation of subjects,
          the very formation of persons, presupposes gender in
          a certain way—that gender is not to be chosen and
          that "performativity" is not radical choice and it's
          not voluntarism.

Performativity is not performance; performance assumes that one has unfettered autonomy over their gender, able to don and doff at will, when in fact gender, for Butler, presupposes one's formation through gender to even *do* it at all; gender has already laid claim in order for one to be said to be a subject that is, as it has already obscured, doing gender. Now, I am no performance theorist, much less a performer, but I do wonder if there is more to be said and salvaged in the performance. Not in the wildly tired and exhausting discourse surrounding drag—the ship for drag's radical liberatory possibilities has sailed for me—but rather in putting on a gender that you do *not* want. It is the phone the dope dealer uses for utilitarian purposes, an ephemeral illicity, to be discarded and thrown in the trash. A burner gender.

Because when one moves through this grocery store, this post office, this sidewalk, and is met with sir or ma'am, bro or dude or giiiirl, there is rarely time—not to mention love and care and safety—to refuse the interpellative gender beck. I do not know you, nor do I know if I shared such intimacies as nonnormative or nonbinary gender with you they'd be received with care, so perhaps I do no such thing and simply wear this man costume like Ralphie wearing those bunny pajamas given to him by Aunt Clara. Ultimately, I don't enjoy wearing it, but when Aunt Clara comes over, expecting me to be wearing this "gift" she got me, and because neither I nor mom nor dad want to spend this time laboring over Aunt Clara's hurt feelings and tears and snide remarks about gratitude and the thought that counts, I wear the pj's. And what do you know, in the wintertime, it can be quite warm. So the day continues, an assumed tacit concession to the validity of the nominatives used to hail. One questions their commitment to the nonbinary, suspects one's fraudulence. But know that that gender is not yours. You don't like wearing the bunny pajamas. And you wouldn't even be wearing them if someone else didn't make you in the first place.

The relationship between you and this body you are said to have is perhaps fraught, perhaps complicated, perhaps used out of necessity because you live in a society that demands you use this form of currency even though you'd rather not, so here you are, playing its game without believing in any of its rules. It's all made up and, ultimately, the points don't matter. To say that this is not my body responds to the assuming of a body with *exhuming* a body with a yearning to dig so deep in the excavation process that you end up on the other side of the world not knowing which way is up. This body you are said to have is always given man or woman, and it sucks. And you don't want it to suck all the time. So, you have some fun. They want you to play this game with these made up rules? Okay then. Let's play—and better yet, let's cheat and break rules and find glitches in the code.

*
**

One of the things about illicit economies, black markets, you know the type, is that they do not spring from pure nefariousness. They spring from economies that have made other forms of economic livability necessary. And since the terms by which one is permitted to live, or kept from not dying, are fixed, many need to find other ways to live in that economy by engaging in practices that subtend the economy's surface. Drug trafficking or fraud or sex work emerge under circumstances that have forced people to be expunged from capitalism proper, which dictates the terms of living—capital, wealth, labor power, marketable skills based on the demands of a market wrapped up in white supremacist cisheteropatriarchy—so surviving requires engaging in other kinds of markets, often termed black markets. (And the racialized language here is not lost on me.)

These economies are under constant surveillance. And they do not exist in another atmosphere, but alongside non-illicit economies. When the narcotics dealer makes calls or appointments, they may not use the same phone with which they talk to their homies. The phone and number they use for loved ones, for fam, may not be the same as the phone used for moving through the economy in which they have been made to move. That phone is not one they have an attachment to. They may use it out of necessity, and they may appear to hold its contours so familiarly, speak and text on it so fluidly. But the feds might be monitoring that phone, its signal pings from the cell towers that impose the user onto its grid. So of course that phone will be discarded, into a bin that the municipality will pick up and recycle for another use.

Masculinity, man—these are, like the device for illicit communication, burner *genders* at times. When I go to visit mom and grandma, I am a son and grandson, baby boy to them. And when the elders back home ask "How you doin' today, young man?" I answer, as I must, "Good morning. I'm doing well, thank you. And how about yourself?" And there is little thrashing. Though there could be, and others thrash because they must. And I will gladly come alongside them, kicking up a storm and raising the ninth circle of hell. But with grandma, with mom, with so many others, I let the "man" stick. That is a "boy" and "(grand)son" with various affects of love and relation attached to it. At any point we are free to dispense with it. Boy and son still remain, still do violence. But with those gendered impositions, there is an attendant—not constitutive—love and care, and perhaps it is those that make the wearing of the gender just shy of unbearable.

And, too, even in those moments of boy and man I am still the one who moves through nonbinariness. I want y'all to know that even when they do not use they pronouns for you or when they actively use he or she pronouns for you, you are no less nonbinary. And still no less nonbinary when you nod along. Because nonbinary is not life in the complete absence of genders that hegemony deems proper to you; there is nothing pure about nonbinariness. Even when one is called sir or ma'am, nonbinary is not negated. We are misread and misrecognized, yes (though recognition is not even what we ought to want, as if being recognized by evil eyes means we feel good about being seen, or *can* even be seen), but that misrecognition *is as important as recognition in the production of self, as the quality of feeling misrecognized/unseen/wrongly viewed serves as a context for the emergence* of the critique of the grammars facilitating violent forms of recognition. And that critique is, precisely, the nonbinary. Indeed, being misrecognized, having the burner genders we have tossed at us lapped up like thirsty gender obsessionists, *carries with it the opportunity for deliberation and the potential rejection of social scripts, which get mapped onto one's body.*[*] You may read us this cisnormative way, and we may concede or nod, say that you've assumed, not correctly, but that I am the one for whom that name, in this moment, fits. But who hasn't been called a wrong name and knew they were still the one being called?[1]

Though, it does feel a little icky, I have to admit. I feel like a poser sometimes. Like a liar. And I know it isn't true, because nonbinariness does not reside solely or primarily in what one is called, or how one decides to call themselves. We don't have to be pure—we can't be pure, as if the validity of our genders and nongenders rests on never having been otherwise. How can you say you're nonbinary if you're not "out" to everybody, if the lady at the restaurant called you *he* and you didn't raise a fuss? Are you *really* nonbinary? If turning at the call makes me feel icky, what makes me feel even ickier is if someone tries to say that I am no longer, or am less, nonbinary having turned.

And also, too, we don't *always* turn. 'Cause it, nonbinariness, is emergent in ways myriad and legion, and in ways subtle

---

[*] C. Riley Snorton

and imperceptible at times. There is a knowing, just for a split second, that I've eluded something in those times when I stand aloof at being introduced to mom's coworker as her youngest son; or when a friend and I are talking and someone else that neither of us knows too well *he*'s me. In these moments there is a pause, and that pause is the sonically mute but affectively stentorian resonation of knowing, feeling, insisting that the pause matters. The pause is nonbinariness inhaling, exhaling, breathing. To sit unresponsive to gender's snapping fingers is to make that self-centered motherfucker wait until you're ready.

Because who, really, *needs* gender? I don't think I want or need it, and maybe you don't either. There is a feeling of protection, like it shrouds you in a cocoon made of a weighted blanket. And, feelings of belonging, recognition, and even joy. I hesitate to suggest that these should be taken from you; I want you to have all that joy and belonging, so there is a bit of timidity in saying all of this. But still, what are we trying to protect ourselves from? What is compelling our search for belonging and recognition; why do we not already feel joy? Is it not that we are trying to in fact protect ourselves from the things we are made vulnerable to by gender—assault, discrimination, overlook, existential circumscription; is it not that we feel that we don't belong precisely because gender has set terms to which we must already adhere in order to belong, such that our nonnormative non-relation to gender has gotten us kicked out of the normative social world that requires belonging on strictly, hegemonically gendered terms? So here's a thought: maybe we are not vulnerable to things that prey on our genders; maybe we are vulnerable *because we've been gendered*.

It is a slight shift, but an important one. We are made vulnerable because gender has happened—if we were not deemed men and women, if we were not inaugurated into the cabinet of manliness to do what it is men must do in order to be and stay men, to proliferate men and manliness, then we would not have to objectify, harm, assume, undermine those who are not men, or who are improper men, or insufficient men, *in order to continue being men.* We would not have to concede that we are women, and those people are not real or true women, so we must exile them because they do not meet the criteria we have established for women, and since we are real women we must remain protected from those who are not real women, and in our real women space we circumscribe all the other ways we might be ourselves because were we to open that up we'd be, alas, more vulnerable. To deem gender of ourselves and others means that we are now exposed to gender being what we mean. And the most profound violence is never being able to mean anything other than what we've been told we can mean.

That is why I want us to give a little bit more love to ourselves, to nonbinariness. It insists that we mean something else, anything else, in this world that has said we can only mean this or that.

*
* *

But sometimes, even though you move through your nonbinariness fiercely, and you think of it—because it is—as your (dis)orientation to the world that continues to make gender a thing when you vociferously need it not to be the thing that it never was and never could be for you, you find yourself gripped up by the world's gender. It sinks its teeth in, refusing to let you go. It is the cinematic bully, holding you up by your shirt collar demanding your lunch money, making you do its homework. You could thrash, sure, and oftentimes you want to, you need to, but the thrashing exhausts you. And are we not constantly exhausted by having to swat away gender at every turn? Sometimes you just want to get this over with and go home.

So you've orchestrated an ensemble of a gender that gets you from here to there. It is not something you own, nor is it a treasured heirloom you bring out on the most special of occasions. You feel very little for it. But it's that pair of shoes, beaten and tattered, you wear to take the trash out, that you slip on to trudge through the mud pit in your backyard after the heavy rain last night. You'd prefer to be barefoot always and forever, and you know that you are no less a lover of being barefoot if you put on that old pair of Reebok that don't even fit you because you're about to wade through twenty yards of sticks and rocks and grime. You sometimes throw on a gender real quick because it could insulate you just a tad from the conditions you are about to go through.

*
**

See, what seems behind all of this, or in front, or coeval, is the indispens-, indisput-, and indisposability of gender as constitutive of personhood. Of, too, sociality. Doing and being gender is perfunctory, it cannot not be there, sitting, watching, controlling, dictating. It must electrify our nervous system and contort us in legible and demanded ways. You can't not do gender; you can't not be gender. So many bring it, gender, to the fore, without a thought; and so many make it unavoidable for those who wish to run from gender, those who wish not to even understand gender as having the right to live here. Even when we try to flee, gender is brought back. This pall of a shadow that hangs there even when I move away expresses clearly that this thing is over between us. Yet it keeps getting brought back. Why?

Even those who seek flight in the most radical of ways at times do not presume gender as a site from which to flee. Those of us who imagine and try to emerge into another kind of world or another kind of relation to and as ourselves in this world also, too, fall victim to bracketing out gender as part of the behemoth needing to be gotten away from. When Arya Stark—and my goodness did I love Arya in that two-year span of being forced to watch *Game of Thrones*—when Arya wants to become faceless, literally rebuking all forms of a static identity, nevertheless it is always, *always* "A *girl* has no name." That "girl" shadows Arya, shadows so many others. Arya, and Jaqen H'ghar, know well that names are not freeing. The proliferation of this name and that name for genders does not solve the problem; names, gendered or not, but especially when those names index gender—and when we note that gender itself is a kind of naming—limit, for to be

given a name is to be fixed into a violent social relation; it is to
be interpolated into a structure of surveillance and control, it
*limits the unnamed, which is to say, the infinite. It is a way of
turning the unspeakable into something digestible.*[†]

It is only revelatory of the limits of language, or the ways
that language, too, has been deputized by cisnormativity to do
its bidding. I love language, love words, and have long believed
that words matter. I, too, have asked *How can the words not
be good enough?*[‡] But maybe they aren't. The words we have
do such a poor job of describing and caressing the things we
desire. We have no word for one's parent who does not ascribe
to gender, or for the used-to-be-sister who is now nonbinary
of the parent who gestated you but is not a woman, has
identified as a man before but may not be a man anymore and
is playing around with neo- and non-genders. They say that
language, that words and categories, are endemic to the Homo
sapiens species, that we've evolved this language as a survival
mechanism. It is necessary and needed, an innocent tool that,
sure, may have been mishandled but is ultimately a necessary
good. Humans inherently make distinctions in order to make
sense of the world; it's how our brains are wired. But what if it
wasn't? What if there was in fact a way to live without having
to say you are different from me in these ways, and now
because *you* are different *from me*, I make a hierarchy based
on this distinction, and connote that hierarchy in specific ways.
And what rises to the level of distinguishable and noteworthy
is subject to histories of arbitrariness and violence (because
there was a very particular, non-just-brain-wiring way that
skin color or bodily morphology came to be important enough
to incite violence, to become entire identities, to be notable
in the first place *as* a difference to be remarked upon and to
have something very specific and multifaceted done about it).
What if, even if it is—though it's not—the case that our brains

---

[†]Hélène Cixous
[‡]Maggie Nelson

are simply wired to organize the world exactly as it is now, we did something else? I choose to believe, and feel there is good reason to believe, that we are remarkably good at doing things we are not "supposed" to; how inventive we can be, how outside of the purported mold we have become, how *un*natural we always seem to be. Is it not possible to bring those vibes to this question: that *if* we are destined to use and make words, categories, what if we did what we often have done and did something else? To bring it back to the point, what if we, even if naming is in our DNA or whatever, did not?

In what world would it be possible for Arya and the faceless (let us not forget that they are still the faceless *men*) to be nothing, without name, nameless and unnamed, to move like the whisper of a shadow without referent at all, unbeholden to identifying nominatives? Not even gender can stick to and tether Arya to a form of legibility purportedly necessary for Arya's inhabitation, Arya's slick evasion of the fundamental bedrocks guaranteeing maneuverability in this world—an Arya who is maybe not nonbinary, as if Arya would *be* anything at all, but an Arya whose generative movement through the world is facilitated by nonbinariness. Arya as *the only inaccessible blip on a streaming doppler,*[s] uncapturable, off the radar, there but not there on terms other than those of not having to be there on specific terms.[2]

That might be a kind of nonbinary life.

For someone whose nonbinariness has not commonly read to others as androgynous, I still get a fair share of affective puzzlement. But to be sure, that is what nonbinary does when it is not "merely" an expressive androgyny, a term I always find myself internally interrogating, for, I don't know, reasons.[3] Nonbinary is so much more than just how someone identifies, or how someone dresses, or the cool, edgy non-gendered name someone uses, like "Z" or something. (Though, come to think

---

[s]Aesop Rock

of it, Z would be a cool name.) But to write, to think, to imagine, to agitate, to tremor through relationality and spatiality without regard for gender is what might be called a nonbinary way of life. So even if one is not read as nonbinary, whatever that would even mean, to move through life nonbinarily takes its toll on those who can't not think through gender, and who then bring that gendered thinking—even in moments meant to be affirmative and complimentary—to engaging with you.

I received this email, seen months after it was sent, because, apparently, I'm bad at checking emails:

May 20, 2023: XXXXXXX

Email: XXXXX50@gmail.com
Subject: Inquiry
Message: Hello, I find you to be very talented but I am wondering if you are FTM? I hope that it is ok to ask as well?

There is little new about such a phenomenon: trans people being assumed to be perpetually, *a priori* given over to the invasive evaluative gazes of others, our histories and intimacies and anatomies—because is that not what you're asking, what in god's name do your genitals look like?!—on display for your knowledge and assessment. Do you, in other words, physically and figuratively measure up? The phenomenon is one that says you are the arbiter and authority of sexological validity, and you will take it upon yourself to burst in, demanding some answers.

Or, perhaps this is too harsh, a mild trauma response to knowing a history I unduly weave this email into, for perhaps it is not this at all. Apologies, random email Prufrock, for you may be saying from the ether: *That is not what I meant at all; / That is not it, at all.*[1] Perhaps what you meant is it can be a

---

[1] T. S. Eliot

touchy subject, so you are trying in the best way you can to heed that touchiness and ask a genuine curiosity you have without offense. Perhaps, too, you were—though we can critique this, even as it is understandable—trying to make sure I wasn't some cis person trying to make an intellectual and literal buck off of presuming I know about the lives of trans people, sticking my nose where it doesn't belong—t4t and t-about-t and only-t-in-t-spaces-talking-about-t-things-or-even-saying-the-word-t. Maybe this is all just a misunderstanding.

Still ... This is, as your subject line reads, your inquiry? Of all that I've said, all I've written, all I've thought about and learned by the graces of so many other brilliant minds, spanning millions of words and thoughts—a few hundred thousand my own—of all of that: *this* is what you ask? This is the thing that is so important that you just gotta know?

But this random email Prufrock is not the only one. Others enter too, in different ways. They enter to assess, like some kind of corporeal insurance adjuster, making sure your claims to this or that gender are truthful. (My partner has shared with me that they, too, have been asked "Is Marquis a trans man?" like we don't know what you're trying to fish for—am I *really* trans.) And when it comes to the nonbinary, rarely are those claims even able to be truthful. Have you done this thing that would demonstrate your "seriousness" when it comes to nonbinariness? Have you had this or that experience that only a real enby would have? Do you look the part?

It seems this phenomenon—this demand for proof, this insatiable need to interrogate whether I or anyone else is "really" nonbinary or trans—operates like a kind of gendered imperialism. It mirrors a bell hooksian "eating the other," where the dominant framework consumes difference, not to honor or understand it, but to reassert control and validate its own authority. In this case, they aren't just assessing claims to gender; they're feeding off the very act of questioning, using their authority *to* question, a questioning that has as its metric for valid answers a cisnormative manual. The interrogation is the point, the endless demand for "truth" a way to re-center cisnormative logics even in spaces ostensibly open to trans or nonbinary existence. Even in spaces without ostensible men, hooks says, misogyny is still present; a cisnormative imperial system doesn't require cis people to be present—it persists, self-perpetuating, in every demand for legibility or authenticity. I do not know if the random email Prufrock is cis or not, but the logics this person is maintaining, the form of interrogation and questioning, the very kinds of questions deemed askable and desirable to be known, comes deeply from within cisnormativity: all things need to be cataloged, accounted for, ensured as not falling out of code. And if it does not comply with code, code will code it. This is how empire works: it assimilates even what seems to resist it, making room for transness or nonbinariness only on its own terms, as something legible, categorizable, and ultimately consumable.

We are forced into a confessional, needing to announce to the one divinely ordained to absolve us of our sins. And that confession cannot be any ol' confession; we must confess like this, use this language, adhere to these logics and terms and conditions. It must sound like a confession, it must sound true, and to sound true means that it must adhere to grammars already in place—and not of your making—that give a thumbs up or thumbs down to whether it is, in fact, true. So it is not enough for you to simply speak the "truth" because truth has a certain look. Gender is true, at least that is the axiom that goes unquestioned. It is in some ways revised and tweaked—it's a social construct but its effects are real, are true; it has material effects; that kind of stuff—but gender, at base, it is said, is true. So you must account for gender in your life. You cannot not account for gender, as it is there, always, and while you might not *want* it to be it *is*. Gender *is*. Now deal with it.

But I ask, as Michel Foucault has asked, *How much does it cost the subject to be able to tell the truth about itself?* A great deal. And if this standing in confession is a constant, to have to tell the truth of our gender, even when we do not want or have gender, the cost is great. You see, the confession, or alternatively as Foucault calls it, the avowal, is disingenuous from the start. The being or beings who stand in judgment of the confession's veracity care little for persuading the confessor of the unimpeachability of that which is confessed. The aim, instead, is to extract the confession in a particular way, to have the truth expressed in a particular way. And this is a quotidian phenomenon. Confession's constancy, its quotidian lilt, resounds from the juridical trial to the confessional booth, all the way to the implicit calls to tell the truth of your status in the world, your adherence to the world's grammars, your alignment with extant vectors of legibility. And this happens more than once, twice; this happens at every moment at the level of gender. The confession must be "I am a man," "I am a woman," over and over, repeatedly to the sanctioned and institutionalized arbiters (doctors, judges, government documents), and again to others deputized as arbiters (growing children on the playground, peers, strangers, teachers, parents).

The confession is a tool of power that disciplines subjects into coherence. To confess is to participate in a system that values adherence over truth, submission over freedom. The act of confessing gender—to medical professionals, to state officials, to strangers—is less about self-discovery and more about surveillance, about drawing the boundaries of permissibility and deviance. To step outside of the confessional framework is not just a personal act but a rupture in the mechanisms that uphold normative power structures. We don't answer the question "What are you?"—because the question itself is meaningless. What emerges in this refusal is possibility, a refusal that cracks open the space for living beyond the constraints of gendered legibility.

Gender is one of the chief forms of inhabiting the world as a subject, which implies the requisite to live one's *gender* truthfully, a truthfulness whose probity rests on an adherence to a normative understanding of binary gender. One is also evaluated on the grounds of how their body is rendered legible based on those binaristic, cisnormative assumptions, making even departures from these assumptions retroactively conform to a binary codified as legitimate through a normative evaluation of gender-potent corporeal sites. In other words, if one identifies as, say, a trans woman, even if the evaluator is supposedly "cool" with such a gender identification, you best believe that trans woman better *"look like"* a woman—feminine, unadulterated, and deprived of any trace of "male" privilege. And that measurement, always relative to cisnormativity, occurs again and again, the same queries and standards abound. *When did you know you were a woman? Have you had the surgery? Do you feel trapped in the wrong body?* You must say from a very young age, you must say yes, and you must say absolutely. So, you must confess, on their terms, to their questions, always through, nevertheless, the narrowed scope of the gender binary as the authorizing agent.

Yet why must nonbinariness and departures from gender rely on claims to authenticity, to adhering to legibilities deemed proper to nonbinariness, anyway? Gender is what needs to authorize, so departing from it offers the beautiful state of not having to worry about authorization at all, no? To leap away from gender into an openness of daffodils and peonies—that is what we caress in the nonbinary, a moseying away from the tendrils of policing. Why, then, would we want to erect gates and barriers for entry, erect a police state in this openness that has emerged because of an elusive disdain for policing?

I feel, I don't know, defensive. I feel defensive, yes, and I feel the need to make sure all of you, whoever you are, know that it *is* fine to do and feel nonbinary in all these imperceptible ways. Because I remember the pangs of invalidation and faux acceptance of how I move through nonbinary. I remember the moment when having "not done anything" between "identifying" as cis to now "identifying" as nonbinary—an improper and inaccurate rendering of my relationship to nonbinary[4]—was met with a look of incredulity. It was a look that made me feel that my nonbinariness was not real, or that it was not, as it were, nonbinary enough. How hurtful that felt. And it insidiously made me question whether I could lay claim to nonbinary, whether I passed the test—a test, at least in this moment, I clearly did not. I want no one else to ever feel that way.

Because the life nonbinary desires is simply another kind of life. Maybe that's what all this is about. Yeah, we at times capitulate—seemingly—to the powers that be, responding to the sirs and ma'ams, not correcting someone who uses pronouns that "match" our assigned genders. But even though we do this sometimes, whether out of convenience or safety or sheer exhaustion, we are not conceding. We are not letting them win, nor are we not really down for the cause. We fly under the radar, yes, but underneath all that is a world of complexity and breadth. The ones who sir and ma'am us don't know what's under there. They don't even know there is an under. We're not hiding; we are planning, strategizing, caring, loving. We are living. Maybe grandma and auntie and pops don't know that we move through nonbinariness. That's okay, I think. They don't know, and don't need to know. We are not obligated to reveal such marvels to anyone and everyone in order to inaugurate our validity. Why would you demand that of us? And simply because we buckle sometimes under the weight of the imposition of gender does not mean we are weak. These burner genders that we sometimes let stand in for us are not ours. The exchange they facilitate is temporary and it is not of our own making, though we make use of them. We are made to make use of them. Just know that we are not necessarily there when they are; we are somewhere else, under that radar, the Doppler unable to read what's really going on.

These burner genders, like the phone tossed after its use, are not confessions of identity but illicit stratagems. They serve as intermediaries, a dialectic between concealment and connection, offering us just enough to move through the structures that demand legibility without allowing those structures to claim us entirely. They are the decoys of gender, small and transactional, operating within but not yielding to the systems that surveil us. The burner gender is a kind of insurgency, one that acknowledges the constraints of its moment while imagining a world where such constraints could dissolve entirely.

Yet, what does it cost us to wield these burners? To slip into the contours of a gender that is not ours, to make ourselves legible to the machine for a fleeting moment? The cost is not only exhaustion but the double-edged pang of erasure and cunning. On one hand, we are erased, smoothed out into the binary templates we reject; on the other, we are cunning, exploiting the openings these templates leave behind to construct lives that exceed their narrow prescriptions. The burner is not the endpoint, but the tool, one that we ought not love, something we discard not with shame but with the quiet satisfaction of having evaded capture, even briefly. But it is not the end, it is the ephemeral gender we *go through … to get to something wider.*[#]

Maybe we pay that Foucauldian price of avowal: standing in the light of another's gaze, confessing truths we never wanted to claim as ours, tacitly affirming the structures that demand those confessions. But the burner gender sidesteps this avowal; it mutters half-truths to those who demand absolutes, then leaves the room before the sentence can be completed. We've given ourselves a discount on the price, and then hid some stolen snacks beneath our hoodies. And paid with really good counterfeits, confessional Monopoly money. If gender is a confession extracted under duress, the burner is the whispered subversion, the refusal to offer more than what is minimally required. And even that minimum isn't met sometimes. So perhaps we are not gender's subjects, not even its fugitives in the traditional sense, but something altogether slipperier—figures of nonparticipation, ghostly presences that haunt the systems demanding our compliance. And when we momentarily step into their frame, borrowing the sir or the ma'am, the he or the she, we do so not as believers but as saboteurs.

[#]Hortense Spillers

The Evil Triplet

Some spaces feel like they were made just for us, even if we know they weren't built to last. Still, we show up, grateful for whatever holds, even briefly. Some of us were raised in that—where a kind of soft ruin was the invitation, not the end. We inherit so many spells already half broken, already aflame. And still, we gather, calling it joy even when the walls flicker with warning. I've learned to expect the warmth of a thing to carry some smoke with it. The places that first held us often smolder, even as we swear it's safe inside. And it is. But sometimes, we still have to leave, roaming and roving with our band of ghosts.

How could we ever forget that some of those places were trans worlds, and they have loved us? How could we not remember, always, how trans worlds showed us they are—and we are—impossibly possible? That is as close to sacred in this world where the sacred does not exist to me as we can get. When there is a gathering in a home, a basement, an alley, an apartment, a hollowed-out rec center and you show up for the first time ever in your life in clothes and with a voice and gait and swagger you've only dreamed about letting emerge through you—that is something special. No doubt about that. And this is why it has been so hard to come to terms with how even that gathering, this world, too, is not everything.

**

Trans worlds have always loved me. In them, I've *belonged*. But belonging, we must know, is fraught with so much. It was McKenzie Wark who articulated it first to me, a desire for belonging but not an identity, a ravenous trans worlding looking for a way to come together without needing to be anything in particular in order to be, validly, together. I've wondered if this is even what I want, what "my" nonbinariness wants: certainly not identity, that arbitrary and power-infused categorization demanding criteria to determine who is in or out, policing boundaries like—because it is—it's its job, but do I even want belonging? In these worlds where I, yes, in many ways do belong, these trans worlds, still there are at times things missing, a waning thread count in the trans worlds I and others find ourselves living through. I do not call it a community, which is honestly a term I don't really fuck with anymore, for a few reasons.[1] And I'm starting to think I do not fuck with belonging anymore either. No shade at all—I mean that—to McKenzie or all those others, many of whom are friends of mine, who search for and find belonging. If you couldn't tell by now, nonbinary life and living does not need to bolster its own validity by denigrating other things, inversely proportioning its goodness by virtue of something else's badness. Nonbinary life is not life that middle fingers "the" "binary." I'm just wondering if nonbinary wants something (ever so slightly, which is everything) else.

Something, I don't know, something more and less and other than—I don't know, *this*. The words don't work, the words are off and wrong. 'Cause it's not just like we don't want this thing. Not even really sure what this thing is, but I don't want it. Plus, it's not even only about the thing and not wanting it, you know? There is a creeping sense—and I heard this in a comedy routine once that was on in the background as I was, well, writing this—that some might think that "nonbinary" is just creating another binary—you know, between nonbinary and binary. And that's frustrating. That's not it ... and it is it. But it's only it because we are constantly, incessantly subject to the binary such that *in order for me to speak a truer* *word concerning myself, I must strip down through layers of attenuated meanings.*[*] I want to run around naked yet y'all keep stuffing me into coats and shoes and hats, then when I try to take it all off you're like, "Wow, someone is really obsessed with clothes, huh?" Like, no, motherfucker, I wouldn't even be thinking about this—wouldn't be saying I am *not* this—if y'all didn't foist it on me in the goddamn first place.

Nonbinary life: at least at this moment, a constant tinkering with all these scraps and seeing if the scraps can be tossed in the trash. And as you might imagine, that could require some fancy footwork when there are protocols for proper disposal of garbage, of recyclables, of toxic chemicals, of this plastic versus that plastic, and, of course, when there are laws and fines for littering.

So what does one do? What does one think? How does one write their own story? There are ways we are marked as a matter of existential course; we are marked in order to properly exist, as to exist in this world validly one must be markable, one must be readable to the world's grammatical structures. Nonbinary life is an attempted excess of that marking, not a belonging to that marking; it is an *[impossible creativity] which ~~belongs to~~ [exceeds] the structure of every mark*[†] in a swamp of the same old scripts; it wants something else and, through that wanting, that unrealistic yearning and insistent exploration, it opens up meaning to … I don't know.

In 2004, Susan Stryker wrote a short but powerful essay: "Transgender Studies: Queer Theory's Evil Twin." In it, she makes the case that queer theory is born from a union of sexuality studies and feminism. As such, transgender studies is queer theory's twin, an evil one because it has the same parentage—that of sexuality studies and feminism—yet is not

---

[*]Hortense Spillers
[†]Emilio Carrera

talked about, locked in the basement, and troubles the pristine familial narrative of the happy, unproblematic family structure (homonormativity, anyone?). (I'll also say that Susan very lovingly and very rightly put me back on the queer and trans historical track when I tried to get way too fancy and said that trans studies was queer theory's "demonic spawn," implying that trans studies came *after* queer theory rather than being coeval with it. Thank you for that lesson, Susan.)

As a subject of analysis and, too, as an analytical subject, gender is left aside in much of the history of queer theory, as it privileged talking solely about sexuality, even though gender is how sexuality gains its meaning—what is sexuality but specific arrangements and convergences of erotic desires through and on gender? (Though it remains that this need not be the case, and is, if you think about it, a little strange that it is the case.)[2] Queer theory, for Stryker, was incredibly hospitable for those doing trans work, but had not, in its intellectual foundation, done *its own* work through trans.

And here I am, feeling so, so similarly, but of a different generation. I was not around, not even alive, for that heyday in queer theory, with all the cool kids doing cool queer kid things. But I was here for some of the later parts of trans studies' emergence. And what an honor it has been. Trans studies is and has been the most hospitable place for me to do and say the things I have been out of my mind enough to do and say. And I've been loved all the while. There is no malice here, no shade being thrown or bones being picked. I have been here for a while—almost a decade, now that I think of it, which is wild—and I would never trade that time. Yet, I've been here for a while, and now I am packing up my bindle and tipping my cap, off on another journey. I'll see y'all at the next gathering, and I'll have some stories.

This is the spirit in which I want this understood. The "this" being how perhaps it just might be that trans studies is not where nonbinary can or should (only) do its work. It is not a disavowal but an experimentation with something else, because there have been protocols and paradigms and guests and cousins that I don't think nonbinary really wants to associate with.

So like, for example—and, I don't know, I might be reaching ... maybe, maybe not—we have gender expansiveness as a hallmark of queer theory's evil twin. Gender expansive folks is somewhat often used to denote trans people. But, like, expansion is literally the language of colonialism, is it not? (I know we don't mean it in that way, but maybe the implication is just strong enough to invite some rethinking.) Just manifest destinying over all these unsuspecting genders out there living their best life before we come over and claim them as our own. Or, this constant tendency to do that thing that a bunch of marginalized and subjugated populations do, right: we've been denigrated and oppressed, so we're going to put our thing down, flip it, and reverse it, and say that the people indexed to the enactment of oppression—important oversight: *not* the oppressive structures and discourses and histories, but all the people who might benefit from that structure, discourse, and history—are actually what is truly bad. So in a roomful of awesome trans people, almost immediately you'll hear how cis people don't get it, are trash; cis people don't think or know or feel; cis people this, cis people that. But if we are in the black-market-small-business of troubling gender to the point, at least, of critiquing the assumption that we know another's gender by making recourse to the visual—like, this is literally what a radical trans politics does: asserts *that one should not readily imagine that gender, in this instance (or any, for that matter), can be adjudicated by making recourse to the visual*[‡]— and yet here we are, so, so sure that we *know* the limits and contours of cis people as fundamentally, clearly distinct and legible from trans people. Or, how the field and the people in the field of trans studies sometimes, not all the time and not all of them, think that simply saying that trans women (and some racialized iteration thereof) are the most important, should be centered in every and all things, are not getting enough lip and actual service is enough. How many times have I—have

---

[‡]C. Riley Snorton

you—listened to someone critiquing whatever and whoever and use as a metric for their own good politics how much they talk about the plights of trans women, black trans women, poor trans women, Marsha P and Sylvia Rivera? I am good, it goes, because I know these people, talk about how these people should be talked about more and used as the coal mine canaries for whether someone is sufficiently on the right side of history; you are less good to the extent to which you do not constantly, incessantly use trans women as the standard for anything you talk about. I'm being hyperbolic, but only a little, I think.

Or, how much purchase is placed on lived experience. This is not new or specific to trans studies and trans people, of course, but I feel similarly about it as I have elsewhere.[3] So it goes: I am this kind of person with these kinds of experiences that hearken back to the kind of person I am. Therefore, anything I say about these kinds of people or this kind of topic—which I am conflating with, making reducible to, the kind of person I am and the kind of experiences I've had based on the kind of person I am—is the truth, is right, is, effectively, bulletproof. (Though we're not here to fire shots, to be clear.) Trans life and trans studies, I've often seen, has gained its validity and its force by asserting that what trans people say about their lives and experiences—and about transness itself—is true *by virtue of* trans people saying these things about themselves. It is, in short, the power of lived experience, testifying that such and such has been one's experience and, therefore, case closed forever.

But, like Cressida Heyes says, *I am also wary of the impulse (including the feminist impulse) to treat testimony as unimpeachable, as if it did not have (and gain) meaning by appearing on to a particular political stage, always in a long-running drama.* What this trans person says about their lived experience is always wrapped up in what is sayable about trans life, what kind of moment we find ourselves in, a moment that always permits or does not permit certain things, which forces us to structure our lived experience into its grammars—grammars that are often limited, violent, suffuse with so many archival scars and keloids that don't really let us say what we don't even know we want. It's this assumption, so pervasive, that experience is only an origin of political truth, rather than being the product of an already-existing politics, a politics that has done the very violation that your approach to (your) trans is trying to combat. What is lived is not an unmediated field subject only to the unfettered and true-blue language we give to it; no, to say something as simple as "Being trans is valid" or "Being trans is beautiful because we can do whatever we want with gender" brings with it so many already-accepted terms and conditions— what "beautiful" even is and how it registers to someone as a hierarchized aesthetic standard over and against other things, an acceptance of gender as needing to exist in the first place and unable not-to-be, a concession to there being verifiable criteria for something to even be valid which then implies that there is an arbiter for that criteria to deem things valid and not valid. The terms are already accepted, tinkering with how to fit inside the terms seen as the pinnacle of what we do in trans studies. And that's awesome. I love that for you.

It's not what nonbinariness is here to do.

Nonbinary, the evil triplet born six and a half minutes apart from trans, *will be the disorder to the terms you have created.*[§] Nonbinary does not care much for touting the unimpeachability of its lived experience because what purchase does the experience that is lived have when the world and people constituting that experience are stuck in the same ol' mill of gender? Lived experience is language used as an explanatory device; trans, it seems, has needed to explain itself. Nonbinary, I want to offer—*not* as a dis but as the sound of the dap of two siblings leaving each other after having an amazing evening of laughter and reminiscing—does not do this. Nonbinary, instead, says *surely I need not explain*

[§]*Bixa Travesty*

myself for you to understand why on an anatomical level, I am breaking up with everything.[1]

Or, and this might be specific to me, maybe, how *full* of gender the field is when I, in trying to live a nonbinary life, am trying to be gender*less*. Maybe this is the kicker here: queer theory's evil twin, super-duperly understandably, loves talking about gender. Gender is tinkered and played with, talked about constantly (I mean, it's in the name: trans*gender*), emphasized, used as a primary identifier and mode of coming together with others, felt as the vector through which erotics and desire move. When we go to gatherings or conferences or just kick it over food and TV, it's gender, gender, gender. It's the thing holding us together, because historically and contemporarily it's the thing that has kept us apart.

So it is now the case that that evil twin's concerns are not the concerns of the triplet. The evil triplet, nonbinary, arrives already detached from the insistence on gender's centrality. It's not here to play in the sandbox of identifying, renaming, or even reconstructing the walls of gendered experience. Nonbinary is less interested in rewriting the terms of legibility, less invested in asserting its recognition on the terms provided by trans discourse or queer theory—that is, gender's centrality, sexuality's centrality. Gender will not be recalibrated or rescued. And nonbinary will not explain itself.

If gender is the mode through which trans and queer studies articulate their politics, nonbinary asks why this even needs to be the mode of engagement. It offers a fundamental question that doesn't merely challenge the assumption of what gender is, but whether gender *should have ever been*, in the first and last place. It is, perhaps, a move not to clarity but to *chaos*, a relinquishment of the frameworks that have held us captive to gender's continuous and relentless reign over our, well, everything.

*

* *

---

[1]Brontez Purnell

Because what needs gender, first and foremost, is the state. Gender allows the state to function. It is not simply that the state "recognizes" gender; it invents and enforces it. Gender is one of the key technologies through which the state renders subjects legible, governable, and manageable. To govern is to categorize, to sort, and to administer. The state makes its work easier by placing us into these bins, these fixed identities that we must carry as though they were natural to us. Whether through the assignment of sex at birth or the bureaucratic rituals of identification— marking "M" or "F" on a driver's license, passport, or birth certificate—the state demands gender not as a reflection of who we are, but as a way to exercise power over us. The abolition of gender, then, is not simply about disliking its cultural trappings, like the pink-and-blue dichotomy or patriarchal roles; it is a refusal to relinquish our ambiguity, our boundless possibility, to the systems that benefit from our containment.

Nonbinary's noping out of gender seeks to disarm the state of one of its most insidious tools. When we cling to the neatness of gendered categories—cis, trans, or otherwise—we inadvertently bolster the state's project of governance. Even well-intentioned recognition of trans identities within the existing framework of gender often risks becoming co-opted into this machinery. For the state, recognizing trans people can become a way to expand its control rather than to loosen it. The inclusion of gender markers like "X" on IDs, while a small victory for some, ultimately reinforces the legitimacy of the state's authority to categorize us all. Why must we be named by it, identified through it, surveilled via it? This isn't freedom; it's the state's ability to stretch its tendrils further while still tethering us to a framework of recognition that forecloses other kinds of possibility.

And yet, we cannot disregard that some of our trans kin want and need gender right now. Not everyone is in the same place in this journey of unmooring. For many, gender remains a life raft in the turbulent waters of cisnormative violence, a way to find shelter, affirmation, or even survival within a world that is still profoundly hostile. This does not negate the larger abolitionist dream; it simply means that the journey is uneven. The work of abolition is not to impose a timeline or dictate how people must navigate gender—that's a teleologic best left to chrono- and cisnormative demands—but to create the conditions where no one needs it to survive anymore. If some need gender to feel held, affirmed, or safe, we honor that. For now. Because the ultimate horizon of abolition is to move beyond even that need.

So, maybe the question is not whether gender "works" for now, but why it exists at all. What would it mean to refuse to grant the state the power to name us? What would it mean to live as blurs, as constellations of possibility, refusing the borders and boundaries that gender seeks to impose? The abolition of gender is not simply about individual liberation—it is about dismantling the structures that have made gender feel necessary.

For a while now, any time I'm asked for a bio, I share some version of this as an asterisked note to the parenthetical that always follows my name—("they," or any pronouns)— depending on the requested brevity or protraction:

> *Note on pronouns: The "preference" for they/them pronouns to describe myself is an attempt to mark my irreverence toward the gender binary, and to mark my tentative and always-in-process relationship to gender nonbinariness. Put differently, this is not to say I "am" nonbinary but, more pointedly, seek a nonbinaristic relationship to my own understanding of my gender—an attempted unrelation to gender, as it were. Thus, it matters less what pronoun one uses for me; I am, ultimately, pronoun indifferent. That capaciousness is simply another attempt to express an irreverence and disdain for the gender binary and the ways it might inhere in pronouns.

Irreverence is a word I've been coming to a lot recently. We are told to revere gender, to worship it and deem it divine, natural, inscrutable at times but all-knowing. It is imbued with such sagacity and allure that to feel at all unenthralled with it strikes many as odd. An irreverence toward gender says that you are not worthy of my or anyone's genuflection.

It is also to say that *being* nonbinary is not quite the pursuit, as if to arrive, once and for all, into the state of nonbinariness means that we're all good now. It is, after all, not a state—with all the nationalistic, bordered connotations therein—or a singular thing that one is. Nor is it some simplistic "just another kind of binary" way of saying one is not binary but this other, opposing thing. I don't want to think nonbinariness as simply the flipside of the binary, though this may betray its terminology. How can I commit to nonbinary as a refusal to even do binaries? Nonbinary as an unrelation to binaristic thinking, to categorization, to the normative?

In this way, it's not about the pronouns, though that is not to say we don't still have big feelings about pronouns and their usage.[4] The pronoun is not where the conversation reaches an apogee; the pronoun, like gender, is not the thing. And to be sure, it could very well be the case that getting your pronouns right is constitutive of feeling loved and cared for. I do not discount that possibility. I suppose what is being said here, if you're willing to hear it, is that I wonder if the pronoun is the only or primary site of gender and its circulating preemption. Is what we want as far as gender and non-gender are concerned reducible to being called a pronoun or might it be something else, something like the erosion of gender as an analytic of personhood in the first, second, and third instance? How, in short, do you move alongside me nonbinarily? And that is far greater than correct pronoun usage.

Maybe what it also is, is that, again, I don't care about gender. They keep saying you should care about gender, that gender ought to matter, that it is all that matters or one of the things that matters most. They keep trying to give me gender, but all this nonbinary stuff is like, "No thank you, I'm good." So what sometimes happens is a turning to they pronouns, because this seems right, for sure, but maybe more fundamentally because it's the closest approximation we have, right now, to not having to answer to gender. They pronouns do some work: it signals to others that I have this kind of non-relation to gender, so I invite you into that non-relation. See, if you are willing, if you might be able to engage with me and others in ways you haven't been able to before, without gender. "They" is an invitation to maybe, for the first time, not have to use gender as a social calculus. The pronouns are not what matters; the pronouns, like gender, are not what I care about. I want you to open up that thick skull of yours and see if you can rummage around and find some cool ways of saying hello, of showing love, of connecting, of living that are not tinged with the residue of gender.

There is often a practice that gets taken up particularly by those marginalized folks who now find themselves feeling gratitude for what they have been gifted to know, where they've been permitted to be due to ancestors or elders or forerunners. There is a genuflection to this relative or this kinfolk, who may seem on the surface hella problematic but ultimately is the reason why I now can speak and live from the position I find myself in. We see it cinematically, where one laments their upbringing or terrible life circumstances, but waves it off, or positively inverts it, saying something like "Those experiences made me who I am today." Or, I've seen it in the intellectual and sociopolitical circles through which I often travel—so, so often it's grandma, who is deemed the most feminist or slyly the most fundamental aspect to one's queerness, even though these kinfolk might be read to others as very much *not*. And to be honest, I truly dislike this practice. I've seen it so much recently-ish—black feminist Mikki Kendall says that her grandmother is *one of the most feminist women I've ever had the pleasure of knowing*; black queer scholar E. Patrick Johnson says that *(almost) everything I know about queer studies I learned from my grandmother*. Yet, these people, like all of us, are complex and troubling in many ways. We need not, I don't think, venerate grandma, or mom, or auntie—why are they always women?—as the only way to honor or love; we can, I think and hope and believe, say that actually, grandma was mad homophobic, mom and auntie are transantagonistic. And maybe I reject and disown them for these reasons. These reasons are the proverbial backbreaking straw such that I wish to sever my relationship despite the ways they've reared me. We can and should say that, sure, these given kin have taught me great lessons, but they also mirrored and enacted the horrific violences of hegemony and normativity; they, too, can do violence, have done violence, and may do violence to me should I fall out of the mold they've accepted—and propound—as gospel.

I believe this wholeheartedly, I do. And yet, I feel the sentiment behind such statements. I feel the urgency to swing in "the other" direction for people whose very lives have been disallowed a chance, whose every move and word has been shot down—literally and figuratively—and whose knowledges have been deemed anything but the rich epistemic trove they are. But we need not do this move. Yet, the move makes sense.

I feel this impulse too. But I want you, reader, to know that you can say that your auntie, your grandmother, your mother is trash. I want you to know that you can and should say that the given family you found yourself thrust into need not be the best or loved or defended. You owe them nothing you do not wish to give them. The inch they may have demonstrated in that fleeting moment need not become a mile for the sake of historical reparation. That inch can be precisely that measurement—one inch. And it can be woefully insufficient.

I've felt this impulse to venerate my mother and grandmother, to say that they are the smartest, most ethical, most politically astute thinkers I've ever encountered. I've told audiences and friends that because my grandmother made this or that passing comment, she was a clear-eyed abolitionist; and I've said that my mother, as she refused to explain her rationale for making a demand of me, was citing a litany of ancestors. But honestly, I do not need to say these things in order to honor them. And, I no longer believe them. My mother and my grandmother, like so, so many of us, are flawed and imperfect, are indeed insufficient and inadequate sometimes, and at other times are quite troubling, cruel, nowhere near enough. I can't clip my relational horizons by saying that these all-too-human people are godlike. So I won't.

Or not just my mother and grandmother, *Tía* too. I cannot forget *Tía*, who I am growing to love, who, too, is imperfect and not enough. *Tía* calls me, and likely will always call me, as her god that I reject commands, *hijo*. *Tía* is 62-years-old now, and she raised four marvelous children. I have not known *Tía* very long, and I still cannot have a full conversation with her. My Spanish is still progressing and her English, while better than my Spanish, is still not tight enough for us to have a robust conversation. And she does not even know that the person who sits across from her—me—calls themselves *they*, that they are *una persona que no tiene necesidad, deseo o interés en un género*.[#] And still, she makes meals with vegetarian options for me, she worries for me, cares about what I think, and calls me family, as if this, too, is a kind of language—maybe the first one we ever shared. And amid all of this, she, too, is not doing enough.

I think it is important to be able to say these things and say when all the aspects of the worlds we move through are not enough, rather than saving ire only for the usual, big bad suspects. Yes, our loved ones, the identificatorily marginalized, ought also to be told they too have work to do. It does us little to insulate them from critique and harsh yet honest words. Nonbinary life, I want to submit, does not cordon in order to preserve an aspect of the status quo because that status quo has wrapped itself in the language of care, of family, of survival, and asked us not to look too closely. But we must. We must, especially, when love demands silence about the injuries we carry from its architecture. We demand still because even tenderness can become tyranny when it asks us not to name what hurts. We feel like we need to honor and protect in this

---

[#]Alan Pelaez Lopez

way, but we do not need to. I promise. We so often defend gender because it's been sutured to the love we feel. But we can and should and deserve to feel love in other ways, in grander ways not affixed to the ways gender limits and qualifies love. We accept a kind of love lacking in so much, disallowing ourselves the breadth of affection ungoverned by normativity. And then we call that compromise maturity, or realism, or family. But I want something else—something lovelier, more dangerous, unshaped by the hands of gender. Something that doesn't ask us to dress up ruins and call them rituals. Because these evil triplets that we are, occupational ghosts and wizards, are sitting with our faces illumined by the village's embers.

Part III

A ~~Man's~~ World

Just because we are in the same room does not mean that we belong to the room or to each other.
—Lauren Berlant, *On the Inconvenience of Other People*

I tried to learn French and wasn't in a good spot to do so. The pronunciation of the French /r/ sound took way too long to learn, and the frustration over why on earth half the letters in this word aren't even pronounced never subsided. The impetus to learn French came from my love for French philosophers. It was my training, and will likely always be a part of the way that I move through thought.

There is this concept one of these French philosophers adapted from someone else, a German philosopher, and which has long intrigued me. The concept of *sous rature*, or "under erasure." It is a concept that puts a term under erasure, literally crossed out, because it is inadequate, problematic, yet, it is felt, necessary. The term under erasure is discarded, but not all the way; the term is stricken from the ledger, but you can see the shavings and faint graphitic hue of its having been erased.

So when I think of *sous rature*, under erasure, I think about all the ways a word tries to mean what it means, but falls short, never only meaning what it tries to mean, and always relying on other things for its meaning. If Martin Heidegger, from whom Jacques Derrida differed in understanding *sous rature*, asks "What to do about the Being that presupposes the definition of Being?" which gets us to his use of the cross-out, I have been asking, through nonbinariness's concerted critique, implicitly at least, of man and masculinity (as well as any particular gender), "What to do about the Man that presupposes the definition, the *only* definition, of Man and of gender?" That is to say, for all those who *man* me and others, what is such a quick, assumedly obvious designation presupposing about gender itself, about what a man is and looks like and does? "Man" stands outside of all outside forces, being obvious and true all on its own, with no support, no history, no inconsistency, nothing other than an assumption of itself as thoroughly natural and simply there. What does a man look like; can you detail that, knowing full well that as you enumerate there will be many "men" who do not stack up to the myriad criteria, many nonmen who will, many assumptions you're bringing in—chromosomes, genitalia, behaviors—that you quite literally have never observed yet are saying that it has gone into your criteria? For "man" to stand on its own, needing no help from anyone or anything, simply *being*—springing, that *lucky guy, from the imaginations of liberal theorists as a full adult, without relations, but equipped with anger and desire, sometimes capable of a happiness or self-sufficiency that depended on a natural world preemptively void of other people**—there are surely a lot of contortions you seem to be doing to make it all stand erect.

Putting man under erasure, then, as ~~man~~, gets us to think about man as never standing on its own, always propped up, and further, always saying something in addition to what it is trying to say. ~~Man~~ is a sign, but a sign to nowhere: part of it implies an attachment, but that attachment does not, in fact, attach; and part of it *always "not there" and ... "not*

---

*Judith Butler

that."[†] To impose "man" in the end doesn't really say much of substance—there is no coherence, no consistency, no accurate and reliable indexing of these or those privileges, these or those characteristics. ~~Man~~. While it touts that it is the all-seeing gender eye, its vision is greatly blurred.

Which is all to say we're kinda just circling around cisnormativity: the ways that cisness—*the biologizing ideology that these social roles of sexual difference adhere to assigned sex based on the appearance of genitals at or (via prenatal imaging technologies) before birth; the idea that those identified as girls at birth are naturally inducted into the social expectation that sexual difference sets for the feminine and likewise for boys with the masculine*[‡]—rules our interpersonal grammars. In this society, one is assumed cis until proven, invasively so at times, otherwise. And there is no otherwise. You are a man if you "were born" a man, the passive construction here cleverly removing any human intervention in this classification. Just whoops, there you are, born'd, and I'll be damned, you are a boy. What this does is naturalize sex *as* gender, matrimonially linking them, collapsing them. And with this, you are doomed to only ever being what you've been assigned.

It might be that even in other, purportedly more open and loving spaces, cisnormativity still operates; there is only and can ever only be two genders, really. Because when thinking about being assigned gender and then moving not to the "opposite" gender but to something else, the transition is deemed incomplete, not sufficient enough, still locked in a binaristic logic because one can only get sufficiently outside of male privilege when one goes to "womanness" and thus rebukes "male" privilege. Anything less is insufficient and still on the assigned side of masculinity, no matter what you claim. The critique of masculinity, of femininity, of gender that nonbinariness levels is deemed disingenuous if you don't run to "the" other side,

---

[†]Gayatri Spivak
[‡]Emma Heaney

as if a true critique means you don't look masculine, as if true not-this can only ever be looking unequivocally like that other thing. Gender critique, then, becomes a box-checking exercise, a form of cisnormative logistics that formulaically necessitates that this plus that plus these equal only what it says those things can mean. The yield is already predetermined; there is no other formula, no other possible result but this. Cisnormative logistics will not grant anything outside of its logics.

But we still ask: what if we (un)do a form of logistics that cannot be quantified or known in advance, a logisticality that exposes the limitations of the frame trying to capture us? Can we not—and I think we can and do—become a kind of misfit that makes no concession to the function and efficiency that cisnormative logistics demands? In such a reading, we're not aberrations to be corrected, but rather the figures who reveal the fallacy of a system (or cistem) that pretends to totality, revealing that its completeness is always incomplete, that its stability is an illusion.

What underlies the return of male privilege to me is, I think, an unspoken assumption that there are true, real ways to be a gender. Sure, they say, you identify as nonbinary and that's cute and all, but to most other people you're *really* a man, and *that* is what matters. They assume the veracity of others' perceptions and cisnormative ascription—in short, they give primacy and first order legitimacy to cisnormativity. And that hurts. To give primacy to what appears to prevailing logics is to also give primacy to a normative sense of materiality and material conditions—that is, the flesh and blood, the concrete, and the worldly (as opposed to the abstract). This carries with it a sense that what is visible and able to be touched is (1) transparent and unmediated, which is to say is subject to no interpretation or history or discursive framings and is simply there for the knowing; and (2) unequivocally true, real, and that which we should prioritize over all else, for it is the most immediate and fundamental. All of this sees the other-than and that which does not align with the framing schema of the immediately and most readily visible as anathema. Or, in other words, things that fall or run gleefully outside of such logics—logics that genuflect only to what exists here and now under these conditions, that aligns with what the frame says exists—are not real or true or to be given the time of day until the concrete and material are addressed first. Such a logic is normatively cis, that is, is fixated on aligning with the structures that provide meaning to the extant grammar, which disallows trans- and nonnormative grammars of life and living; indeed, that deems such grammars as a distraction from what is most important. This has the effect of rendering cisnormativity more important than radical attempts to opt and break out of this.

That is what I'm trying to get across. Under this heading, there are two and only two genders and you will be treated accordingly, and that according treatment is what truly matters. Meaning, too, that we have an understanding of real gender (man and woman) and unreal genders, and the real genders are all that matter. No matter that living and thinking through the nonbinary necessitates an irreverence to cisnormativity; cisnormativity cannot say that we, or anyone, are truly this or that gender. It is a regulatory apparatus quelling the potential of radical gender abolition, jailbreaking gender, that inheres, in this instance, in nonbinariness. The *you still have male privilege* is a carceral response, a response that locks me, and others, back up despite our joyful escape.

"Man" is such a loaded word. More and less than itself, it is a signifier that brings so much with it, implies so much after it, and in fact says very little at all. On one plane, "Man," with the hubris and parochialism the initiating capital letter evokes, signifies the purportedly universal in humanistic terms: the history of Man is the history of humanity, "mankind." With this comes, as any early-stage feminist can tell you, the assumption that "men" (note my scarequotes here, where they might very well be absent in said early-stage feminist's articulation) can stand in for the general and universally applicable. And what a slight this is. On another plane, we have to turn only to Sylvia Wynter, whose intellectual corpus has painstakingly eviscerated the embedded racialized and gendered reverberations in "Man" as a genre that, in her lexicon, overrepresents itself as humanity. On still another plane, there is a way that "Man," especially when racialized via blackness, is understood differently, as a signifier—one that is assumed simply to be a descriptive articulation of an extant, transparent being—of a certain class of endangered subject given to special considerations (that are, it is insisted, *not* to be conflated with being "patriarchal" or "sexist") or who are in fact the *most* marginalized and oppressed subject par excellence. None of these are appealing.

But still, all of this is murky and bedeviled water in which to wade. On a number of fronts. There is the looming specter of my own identification, which I have spoken to before,[1] and which I will speak to here once more. I am not a "man," nor do I wish to be. Contrary to how the assemblage called my body signifies to nearly all, such assumption of my manhood—which many tout as an ethical responsibility to be claimed and owned, instead of, closer to truth, a profound and coercive violence—is precisely what I reject as the architecture of gender's capture. I want to assert that I refuse manness out of a gesture for gender abolition, out of refusing the very meaning of man and woman, of gender; I want to refuse it because I do not believe that gender can attach to me in the final instance, and refusing manness is the very practice of gender abolition, of nonbinary, and a taking deeply seriously that *one should not readily imagine that gender, in this instance (or any, for that matter), can be adjudicated by making recourse to the visual;*[§] that *the category of sex is a totalitarian one, which to prove true has its inquisitions, its courts, its tribunals, its body of laws, its terrors, its tortures, its mutilations, its executions, its police ... It grips our minds in such a way that we cannot think outside of it. This is why we must destroy it and start thinking beyond it if we want to start thinking at all, as we*

[§]C. Riley Snorton

must destroy the sexes as a sociological reality if we want to start to exist;[1] that *the Nature you bedevil me with is a lie*[#]—I am not, and do not wish to be, and will not be, and do not need to be, a man.

So what I'm thinking about in this weird nonbinary context is how someone would read me, as "man," and then say that the material realities of how I move through the world are that of man—"women" fear you when you walk behind them at night, "other" "men" assume a camaraderie with you so you get privileges from that, you can dress as you do or talk as you do and not have that ding your status because only a man would be able to do that and not have it count against them. This kind of stuff. Who I am *really* is dictated by what the social world (a cisnormative, white supremacist, capitalist one) says of me. What I say, what I refuse about how I am positioned against my will and intentions and imaginations for the future, does not matter. And it is because those aforementioned material realities are more true and real than my imagination. Which leads me to my point: what underlies those material realities, that foundational trueness, is a cisnormative logic that says there is only, really, man and woman, and *you*, Marquis, are the former. Tough.

But I've gotten ahead of myself, because many I've encountered are trying to *redefine* masculinity, men, men and masculinity—it's unclear sometimes where the slippage between the terms happens. But I've forgiven that for now. How to navigate masculinity, let's say, when it has delivered to certain iterations of men—perhaps most iterations of men—a complex amalgam of things, not just one big bad thing. Put differently, what to do with and how to navigate the call by progressive and liberal and even radical feminist men and masculine people to change what masculinity means, and that alone, not to get rid of it or "pretend" it doesn't matter or exist.

---

[1]Monique Wittig
[#]Susan Stryker

Characteristic of this position is Jamie Utt, who has written in "A New Masculinity: Why I Need Feminism as a Man," that the goal is to encourage and *invite men to reconsider what it means to be a man*. Utt's central claim, like numerous others, is that it is key to invite men into a conversation, to call men *in*, Utt says; to note that while masculinity has made pervasive the message of men needing to be emotionally unavailable, physically dominant, sexist, and homophobic, it has also, Utt says in characteristic we-need-to-help-men-see-that-being-a-man-is-okay-and-just-need-to-let-them-know-there-are-other-and-better-ways-to-be-and-do-manhood fashion, instilled in men a sense of strength and brotherhood. Feminism, Utt notes, is not anti-male but anti-*traditional* masculinity. And men need simply to have their fears and insecurities spoken to in order to feel heard and thus more given to heeding feminism's call.

Utt rejects gender abolition—which is to say he rejects the urgent call of nonbinary life—having received a number of emails from people calling for it (me not included). Utt's rationale for departing from a gender abolitionist politics is that he doesn't *find it helpful for meeting most people where they're at*. I must say, this common refrain, which inducts pragmatics in service of valiant, levelheaded political work, is quite vexing. Where "most people" are at is not so much at issue; it is, in the specificity of this treatise, where those who ascribe to and buttress masculinity are at, a distinction and nuance not granted, in my estimation, in Utt's texts or most texts concerning "men." Indeed, many of the things that swirl around the blogosphere and Twittersphere and all the other -ospheres continually conflate men and masculinity, assuming that the bearers and doers of masculinity are synonymous with men, and furthermore, and more importantly, assuming masculinity is an inherent or natural quality *of* the being of a man. From here, the penchant to meet "most people" where they're at—and this "most people" is to be read as those whose politics are suspect—is to me a concerted dilution of the work of those doing the reaching out (and most of their work is, in my opinion, already watered down). Where the people in question are at is typically, quite frankly, trash. Why would I want to "meet" them there? (To make it more likely that they feel heard, folks might say. To be more practical and realistic about what it takes to "convert" people, they might also say.) This pragmatic approach, which is deemed more "realistic," holds a monopoly on what a valiant and sensible response is. But trans people, nonbinary people—indeed, transness and nonbinariness—know something about the joys and imaginations of the impossible. The pragmatic is practical and thus fixated on the structures already in place, fitting in and maneuvering within what is already here. But is not what is already here precisely what we are trying to change? Why fit within it when I am trying to not-fit far, far away from it? Nonbinary life has no concern for the practical and pragmatic, for here, in nonbinary life, *the pragmatism of the present is smashed in the name of a life we might survive.*[**] It is pragmatic and practical to try to find the fire extinguisher to put out the fire on the stove, but who needs that practicality when you have been trying to have the house burned down for years now?

It's not really so much the case that men merely *are* everywhere, but that we *make* men, gender, appear everywhere. A couple years ago, I was watching a video game streamer play one of my favorite video game series of all time—*God of War*—and there is a moment in the original PlayStation 2 game where a titan appears. Titans in Greek mythology are gigantic creatures, ruling their own universes, their power rivaling that of the gods. And this is a video game with centaurs and medusas and magical powers and superhuman strength and, you know, mythical gods. As soon as this titan appeared, you see its full form, and because it's not an X-rated video game, between its legs is a smooth, inconspicuous space. At this scene, someone in the chat exclaimed, "Where's his dick?!" We are about ten

---

[**]Eric Stanley

hours into this classic game, you've seen this mortal become cursed with the ashes of all the people he's killed, fighting myriad non-real creatures, do super- and extra- and nonhuman feats and didn't say a word. But when this particular—again, mythical—creature appears, you just cannot fathom that it does not have genitalia in the shape of what you assume it must have? Even in this world, men must exist in the way you understand men. Gender must exist in this way. Why?

*
**

Growing up boy'd is a wild experience. Growing up X'd in any way is a wild experience, I'm sure. In the specificities of the annals of Philly and its outskirts, being boy'd led to numerous confusions on my part. I guess even then I refused and failed the script, longing—like maybe, just maybe, most of us do—for nonbinary life, a life without the strictures demanded by gender. My growing up was routed through having to be, and being made to do, boyness, and with that came much pain, and, too, some joys. One can never simply *be* when made to grow up through gender, and I so deeply wanted to just be, alleviated of what gender demanded. Even in the joyful moments of my favorite action figures and cartoons, my comfy pajamas, or mom's love or big brother's respect, there it was, gender, setting the terms of that emotion. It was of course the constant chastizations that boys don't cry—which forced me to shame myself, my empathy; and then forced me to hide my tears and develop stratagems for disappearing them in silence, converting feeling into quiet endurance—and there is so much more than could be said of this worn topic. Other, more subtle disciplinary measures under the guise of the protocols of rearing occurred too though: the unspoken praise for roughness and restraint, the way softness was met not with reprimand but with redirection. A small wince corrected into a blank face; a curious glance toward something "girly" met with silence that rang louder than any scolding. These were ontological instructions, rehearsals for becoming someone I never consented to be.

I wanted to be held without instruction, to be allowed to feel my feelings without them being routed through the narrow corridor of boyness, that larval stage preceding manness. Even when I was happy—and I was, I was a happy, gleeful child—my smile too had to be just so, just enough. It had to be there but not too bright or vulnerable, not too delicate. Even joy had rules, even happiness had to wear a gender. As though every emotion needed to pass through a filter before it could exit from me.

This is not to say that I identified as nonbinary back then. Such would be a lie, as well as an oversimplification. In all those moments of feeling myself through gender and being felt by others through gender, I wanted out of a thing, or many things, that required I become a boy first before I could become anything else. I wanted to live a nonbinary *life*. Being gender, being boy'd, does not allow that kind of freedom.

Notice that here we are not saying "growing up *as a boy*" nor "as a young boy" ... or anything like that. The point is to try in as many instances as possible not to assume that we simply *are* a gender. To use the aforementioned phrases, which seems so natural and innocent, concedes that boyness is just a fact about us, impacted by nothing outside of that ontological, existential fact of boy. No one did anything, told you anything, beat you for anything, yelled at you for anything, coerced you toward anything, failed to present other options. None of that. To be boy'd, then, is to in a very small way turn ourselves toward the quotidian decisions of boying: the thousands of corrections and oversights and nudges that keep us in line, on not only this side of the binary but within the binary so fiercely that there is no outside.

I was talking to a group of marvelous people about gender, and trying to get them to come along with the thought that gender *happens*. That is the distinction between "as a boy" (gender *is*) and "being boy'd" (gender happens). It seemed like this group, mostly in their late thirties and early forties, some in their early fifties, and never having been exposed to thinking outside the normative (but incredibly curious about the nonnormative), wasn't quite there yet. So, I tried to bring them along through a scenario that clarified all the tiny decisions and nudges that gender, that gender*ing,* imposes:

Meet Dave. Dave was conceived at some undisclosed time and location, and roughly 270 days later breathed the air of the world we live in. Before Dave even emerged from Dave's gestator, Dave was called *he.* The family in which Dave was reared called Dave *he,* and they did things that they thought they needed to do to a *he:* they bought certain clothing, reacted to others when they encountered Dave as an infant in alignment with what they thought they needed to. They projected a trajectory onto Dave, and made jokes about how much of a "ladies' man" Dave already was, or imagined—and then implicitly coerced—that Dave plays with these toys as practice for the life Dave would inevitably lead, not to mention never, ever allowing Dave to play with other toys that would "confine" Dave to the domestic or to carework. Then Dave began to grow up and maybe started to like the color pink, and saw these pink shoes and wanted them. But Dave's dad said that Dave couldn't get those shoes; it is not the proper color for Dave. Dave saw that pink shoes made Dave's dad unhappy, and Dave felt love from Dave's dad, wanted to keep feeling that love, so in order to keep dad from becoming unhappy, Dave decided "I don't like pink anymore." Then maybe a few more years later Dave wanted to do ballet because Dave saw this incredible person on TV doing ballet and it looked fun. So Dave told some friends, and they started to laugh, because people like Dave, they said, don't do ballet. It's for other kinds of people, who Dave is not like. And since Dave wanted to have friends, and liked these friends, Dave now does not pursue ballet. And then more years later, Dave meets someone who Dave feels amorous desire for. But Dave does not wish to only think about or do sexual things with this person, who the world is saying is the "opposite" of the kind of person Dave is. And then when Dave does not enact sexual rapacity, Dave is made fun of, deemed less the kind of person Dave is said to be, ridiculed. So now Dave decides the next time there is desire for another, Dave will be sure to perform the role *he* is told *he* needs to.

So when Dave says, "I'm just a guy, I just like these things," we should know that to say this obscures the thousands of ways Dave was not allowed to *not* be anything other than "just" a guy. That is how gender happens, I told this group. In the minutiae of life, the quiet moments where gender does not even seem to register. Gender has invaded your desires and your sense of who you are, didn't even ask to stop by, and now has made itself at home. Does that not sadden you? Enrage you? Make you feel lied to? Can you imagine allllll the other things you might have decided for yourself, allllll the other relationships you could have had, ways you could have felt, if it weren't for gender telling you, nope, this is all you get? How absolutely rude and inconsiderate gender has been to us.

A recurring and unsettling thought threads through this project on nonbinariness and gender abolition: how insistently we are pulled into gender's orbit, even when we refuse its terms. Even those who seek no part in its grammar are hailed, positioned, named, and deputized. One can reject manness, renounce its categories, but still find oneself drafted into its ranks—made to stand as man, to be addressed and reacted to as man, especially by those who claim to have stepped outside gender's regime. This is the quiet violence of gender's stickiness, its way of making itself present even, or especially, in the mouths of those who claim to live without it.

How many times have you gone to a friend's, a colleague's, a relative's, and, say, their cute dog barks at you, only for the immediate response to be, "Oh, he doesn't like men." The words flow, seamless and rehearsed, an invocation rather than an observation, as if that which is occurring is not merely occurring but is a deeply profound confirmation of the inevitable. No differentiation, no querying. Obviously, it is because of you being, on untainted animalistic frequencies, a man.

But what assumptions—what grammars—are at work here? *He doesn't like men.* The phrase is simple, yet it is freighted with an entire architecture of certainty. The dog barks at you, and its barks are immediately and uncritically read as a critique of your supposed manhood. No thought is given to the cut of your jacket, the movement of your body, the trembling of your voice; no pause to consider the pitch of your laugh or the unspoken vibrations that might ripple across species lines. Or even the bark at the "woman" that goes written off, anomalous, because surely *that* was just a mistake. Instead, it is decided that this, this *being barked at*, is a testament to masculinity's ubiquity, its indelible hold even when one refuses its jurisdiction.

The dog is weaponized to naturalize gender, a way of cutting through the chaff to get to the heart of the matter. You may think X about yourself, stylize yourself in Y way, but those are categories that other Homo sapiens need to respect out of social convention and politesse. The dog need not perform in this way, and indeed can only be a straight shooter. What "man" is and looks like, smells like, exists as, is universal, with zero variation, a transhistorical and timeless bark with a third eye into the gendered depths of the universe. But would this dog who doesn't like men have barked at your colleague who is five-foot nothing, has short hair, a full beard, dark skin, and was assigned female at birth? Or your friend who is the same height as you, pale as a pasteurized milk, high femme, and assigned male at birth? Or the passerby who is intersex, bearded, long-haired, with a voice several octaves higher than yours? Might you be wrong about your pup? Might your pup be wrong? I mean, we all make mistakes.

To encounter this scene, this barking, is to confront a kind of brutal facticity: not the barking as such but the imposition of its meaning, a *mattering map* through which gender organizes life. The barking is not allowed to remain open, unresolved, unnameable; it must be pressed into the service of certainty. And in that certainty, we see the machinery of gender—its compulsion to name, to fix, to adjudicate—in action.

It feels, in many ways, almost like a script. The frequency with which this refrain—"Oh, he doesn't like men"—appears is uncanny, as though the words have been etched into a collective script and rehearsed for occasions just like this. You'd think, hearing it, that the speaker has heard this refrain before, that it lives somewhere in the zeitgeist, passed down as a kind of folk wisdom. A recitation of received terms, the repetition of truths that have long ceased to be questioned. There is no questioning of its genealogy, no wondering aloud where this notion came from or why it holds. Instead, the words are repeated, borrowed truths passed down like heirlooms, as though one cannot help but affirm their inevitability. And this affirmation, this reiteration of the already-known, shores up the very thing it presumes to describe. The barking dog becomes a soundscape of subjection, its voice enrolled in the project of gender's unending narration. The more it is said, the more true it becomes, until the barking of a dog becomes the blueprint for a naturalized and immutable masculinity. Such is the recursive logic of a world committed to gender's absolutes: it teaches us to rehearse its lessons so well we forget they were ever learned.

Joshua Bennett teaches us, in *Being Property Once Myself*, that animals are never just animals; they are sites of projection, repositories for the anxieties and fantasies of the human. The barking dog, then, is not merely an animal but a node in the vast network of human meaning-making, its sounds drafted into the service of gender's perpetuation. The dog does not bark at you-as-man; the dog barks. The rest—the explanatory edifice—is built swiftly, reflexively, as if to shield the speaker from the terror of ambiguity. Because we ought to know that animals are not merely symbolic. They are living creatures onto which human beings map their fears, desires, and modes of domination, rendering them objects of thought and, simultaneously, something more than that: sites of contestation and potential critique. So it seems that maybe *you* are the one saying that your dog doesn't like "men." And I take grave issue. Fuck that; the dog has said no such thing.

But if it is the case that your dog is barking at what it has said is a man, irrespective of the refusal of gender the subject before it has decided for themselves, then fuck your dog too.

⁎

Y'all get so antsy when it is suggested that maybe we can or should get rid of "man." Y'all try to soften it, say that there are good men out there, that there are millions of ways to be a man, that there is toxic masculinity and then there are nontoxic masculinities. Maybe if we just clean up these edges and give it a nice clean shave, a haircut, some new slacks, and teach it not to use vulgar language, we will be okay. But haven't we already said that man, as gender's apex form, is carceral? The prison bars or guns or fists or threats do not become more acceptable if we give it a new coat of paint, make it pink, write "LOVE" in rainbow colors on the knuckles, or say please at the end. All these attempts to soften man and masculinity is that shit where *people want the administration to take a pay cut rather than vanish or the police to be impoverished rather than never.*[tt]

It's like this video I showed to one of my classes. It was a class on gender and black masculinity, which I confess I dislike teaching. I found and continue to find talking about masculinity a bit boring. It is, frankly, uninteresting—there are so many more things I'd prefer to discuss, like nonbinary life, genderless life, radical politics, rather than starting from 101-level masculinity is bad, your dad is problematic, and your brother is mad sexist. But anyway, the video. It's a thirteen-minute video of a bunch of ostensibly black men discussing how they define masculinity, how they respond to mandates of masculinity, how they relate to other ostensible black men, and how they feel about black masculinity. In some ways it is heartwarming, in other ways it is thoroughly yawn-inducing. One student in the class for one of the essay assignments wrote in part about that video. The student was, like me,

---

[tt]Fred Moten

quite underwhelmed by these ostensible men talking about masculinity. And this student zeroed in on exactly the part—of the ostensible black man who I found the least compelling in the video—that I always found so perplexing. "Masculinity is whatever a man does," the person in the video said. And this student, whose name is MJ, gave a brilliant written response:

> One of the videos in class that made me realize this [that gender, essentially, is bullshit; that masculinity is bullshit] the most was the video where a series of men were defining what masculinity means to them. One of the men said something along the lines of, "masculinity is whatever a man does." But if you make something that expansive, what delineates masculinity from femininity? At this point, you are just dancing around abolition of the gender binary—an abolition of sorts, that is only missing the part where you actually abolish anything.[2] ‡‡

Reading that line hit like a perfect bar in a hip-hop track—you know the ones that force a rewind, that demand you stop and honor the clarity. Because that's it. Every attempt to stretch masculinity until it includes everything is just an effort to save it from critique. Every "what about this version?" or "what if we made it more expansive?" is a bid to keep masculinity intact while pretending it's not doing harm. It becomes abolition in everything but name—gender abolition without the actual abolition. Just say it. Let it go. You'll survive, I promise.

---

‡‡MJ Sasse

Redwoods

"I would love to go to the Redwood National Forest," I said. "For some reason, I've long been obsessed with redwood trees." And I don't fully know why. Maybe because I have never been surrounded by such size without the connotative specter of my own smallness. I don't know. Maybe because I've grown tired of the curation corralling all the other trees I've encountered in my life and wanted to experience trees that seemed so far from that curation and corralling. Maybe I wanted to learn from them how to elude that. And so, the following summer, we went. We spent eight days traveling from Oregon down the coast of California. Our first stop was Portland to visit some friends of my partner's. It was my first time in Portland—in the Pacific Northwest in general—and the weirdness that Portland is known for was evident. I liked the vibe.

Our second day there, after getting our bearings on the first day, we went to Powell's bookstore. We're both nerds and like reading books. We walked away with a hefty stash of bound intellectual worlds in a recyclable bag and made our way to the house of my partner's friend. I'd heard much about him, and I liked him even more once we stepped on his front porch and were greeted with a doormat that said "Go away." As we knocked, his chubby dog, Tony, let the world know that humans were at the door.

We chatted for a while, and his wife came home, accompanied by their five-year-old, and we were gifted goldfish and Legos as we caught up. It was a nice day out too—that is, for the Pacific Northwest, a climate that is as close to literal heaven for me who loves an overcast, dreary atmosphere—so we walked down the street to the community garden, the four of them speaking intermittently in Spanish and me practicing my listening, the weakest of my language learning skills. The community garden was pristine, a testament to something else, some other way of living, being possible. The five-year-old was asked "Do you want to water the plants?" to which the child giddily agreed. And did wonderfully, in the way that little kids do, which is not all that wonderfully.

We said our goodbyes a couple hours later and made our way down the coast the following day. Stops were made for food, for bathroom breaks, for our hotel stay in Neskowin, not far from the Neskowin Ghost Forest. And then, on to the Redwoods. We arrived the following day.

Walking around that forest, you feel many things. And if you're like me, you ask yourself many questions. What, and more accurately who, are these trees, as they are part of the vast ecology of *land who loves us back,*[*] who not what, subject not object. They are beings older than any written history, their roots reaching deep into stories we cannot read but only sense. They are companions to the earth and sky, translators of sunlight into air, anchors of ecosystems that hum quietly around them. They are survivors, witnesses to cycles of life and destruction, holding in their bark and branches the collective memory of what it means to endure. These trees are organismic neighbors, ancestors, guardians, and, perhaps most profoundly, collaborators in a world that is both theirs and ours. Amid this, you feel small, yes, obviously; you feel a sense of calm too,

---

[*]Danez Smith

knowing that this space has managed to elude the bulldozers and capitalist whims of those who would want to "develop" it or colonize its space for condos and mansions and retail. There are no speeding cars here, no rushing back to the office, no hustle and bustle. It's a glimpse of another rhythm of life. And in that there is a reminder that there *is* another rhythm of life, that the rhythms of clock in and clock out, measure up, get in line, behave according to the script, and, yes, of gender need not be the rhythm I follow.

So when you walk along the narrow pathway that maneuvers through this byzantine, nonlinear route through a cumulative millennia of bark and leaves and life, you cannot help but know that there are other ways to do this life. Between and amid the pictures taken, the literal tree-hugging—and you of course ask the trees for permission before you hug them—and the upward-looking to the point where your neck begins to hurt, you notice that something is different. There is another kind of world here that does not operate in the same way. You begin to notice that you are small compared to these sequoias, which in the other kind of world that is not this world would immediately launch you into thoughts of domination and comparison, that these trees could crush you, that you are inadequate relative to these trees. No, now, you notice that you are being held by these trees, by this forest; you are being nurtured by these trees. You can breathe so deeply—and breathing, you've known since May 25, 2020, yet so much longer before that, is crucial—because these trees exhale your life. They ask not for reciprocation, for return on their investment in you; they ask for nothing but to be here with them. Welcome.

Because you see, in that forest they make no demands of you. You do not need to meet a criterion—where we entered into the forest, there was no gate, barely a sign letting us know that the road to the pathways was there. We parked over a mile before the first path because we simply did not wish to force the forest to bear the weight and upkick of a car's tires. So we tread lightly on that earth. And it did not demand we do that; it invited us in, without criteria or restraints, and we felt loved by that. We felt invited to care differently, because we were cared for differently. The forest, to bring this more to the point, did not ask of us to verify ourselves in order to enter or to stay or to wander. It did not demand that we wear this or stay only for this long. Nor did it ask me to answer for myself—who I was, what was my business there, where's my ID. It asked me nothing. It only said, again, welcome.

I wonder what life would be like if that welcome was stretched so far as to be scary. Because nowhere else, really, have I felt so unconditionally invited. Everywhere else I go, there is this seeming expectation that I adhere to something, and so often one of the somethings is gender. There is a ritualistic recitation of gender's catechisms, a demanded genuflection to the binary, or to queer icons, or to what others think is sufficiently trans or androgynous or any other criteria. Even when it is there in a radically altered way, it is nonetheless there.

But not with the Redwoods. With them, there is the enactment of another kind of sociality.

The Redwoods did not ask me to account for gender. There was no box-checking with those trees. I texted pictures of those trees to my dear friend, nonbinary and one who loves communing with the outdoors, where the outdoors is outside in and with what is called "nature" but also where the outdoors is a form *of social life exceeding the racial, sexual, gendered, economic, and neurological protocols of self- and civic administration and of the normatively human.*[†] That friend, the most beautiful soul on this planet, said, "Those trees surely hold the wisdom of old gods." And while I do not believe in gods, nor do they in any normative sense, they are right: those trees hold a profound wisdom. That is wisdom that has no concern for trifling matters such as gender and adherence to its narrow scripts for social viability. They have much, much else they've deemed, in their wisdom, far more important.

The Redwood trees were perhaps the first entities on this planet who—again, *who*, not *that*—upon first meeting me did

---

[†] J. Kameron Carter and Sarah Jane Cervenak

not need gender to make sense of me or my context. I was not dragged into the mandates required by other spaces in order to validate my existence; indeed, that these trees did not force upon me a mode of living that I did not wish, that they did not even register such a mode of existing as a matter that mattered allowed me to exist in another way. They did not need gender, nor did they need gender from me. They asked for something far more important: can you be here with us, for as long as you'd like, simply being? And I ontologically wept.

There is no grand political action plan here. I am sorry, if I may break the literary fourth wall, that I have not given you, reader, something actionable here. I am sorry that I have not told you step-by-step what you can do. There is no immediate plan of action here. And while I am sorry, I want to refuse this impulse of the immediately applicable. One of the things nonbinary life does, in addition to it being staunchly, unapologetically, steadfastly politically oriented—oriented in a profoundly political way in that it orients us away from this world and insists on another kind of world the implication of which is a critique of this world's grammars—is simply, merely letting us all be. It is *an interruption into the political demand for the immediate political applicability of feminist thought*,[‡] of trans and nonbinary thought. We know the refrain, that the personal is political. It is. And here, now, it might not be, not because we are growing tired of all the politics or think politics has no place here. That's not it. Nonbinary life has bigger fish to fry, or different fish, or no fish at all, just nourishment that is not predicated on the cessation of other life. To live with the nonbinary, and that which perhaps makes a nonbinary life, is to yearn for a life that does not tie its meaning to that which seeks its eradication. It glimpses the profundity of having done so much work that now, after all the work, there is nothing left to do but be here, with everyone, everything, and everynothing else.

[‡]Robin Weigman

There is so much that we've received that we don't know about, that has permitted us literally to live in the ways we are able. There is so much wisdom that constitutes us, that constitutes me. What a profound gratitude I have for even being able to exist, here, right now, on this planet with so many other entities that have said, in myriad ways, just be here too. Like the redwoods.

NBFFs (Nonbinary Friends Forever)

Growing up as a shy kid in Philly was … interesting. In myriad ways, absolutely, but perhaps most particularly—and most relevantly for this meditation—in terms of making friends. I had friends, a lot of friends, maybe too many for me, actually. Some of them I garnered from school, some from the general neighborhood, and still more from those who knew or knew of me—I was Gee's (my older brother, government name "Gordon") little "brother" or the kid in high school in the 1,000 lbs. club. All of these friends, though, were quite eclectic. The ones I gathered on my own were an interesting bunch; they were indeed that: *interesting*. I moved with folks that someone like my brother, the aforementioned Gee, would never move with. They were even folks who would not move with each other—white kids who listened to metal and alternative rock, who greatly broadened, beautifully, my sonic palette; nerds who introduced me to shows and video games that were never considered a possibility in our household, who read books and went to cosplay events; punk girls who dyed their hair weekly and with whom I could have conversations that did not have to have any air of ulterior sexual motive; hardcore Philly dudes who smoked grape Swisher Sweets and stood outside of corner stores for hours.

These people resonated with me in a whole bunch of ways, and I like to think that I resonated with them. Why? I'm not sure. But I wondered then, and certainly wonder now, if it is possible that the reason was something ineffable, or a certain disposition toward dissent and proprietary escape and finding generative coming-together on grounds emphasizing breaks or breaches from normativity, from decorum and propriety. And it seems to me I've been forging relationality and indeed subjectivity with myself and others on those grounds, rather than other grounds understood as more proper.

What, though, were those other grounds? Or, perhaps they weren't grounds at all, instead the vitiation of grounds and an insistence on livability, on flourishing, when one floats without the sediment of grounds. My friendship was and kind of still is about something else that may in fact not be rightly considered that which friendship is typically predicated upon. I mean, if I'm being honest—and I am—there has long been an expectation and, indeed, requisite that my friendships and relationships, my communities and people, be predicated upon who else bore the same gendered ascription, gendered imposition as I; the same racialized identity as I. And it has long been hard for me to refute those assumptions, for numerous reasons. It is something that still rears now, even, though in different hues (literal and proverbial) and with different impulses and intentions.

Perhaps I want different criteria or no criteria at all. Perhaps I just want an alleviation of needing to pre-vet how I come together with others. We need not know that right now, or perhaps ever; or, we *can't* know that now and when we do come to know it or are gifted with an understanding of it, it may be a world in which we forgot this was even a question to ask. But in the interim, or rather as a means by which to move in that (non)direction, it is going to be necessary to disarrange our relationality. So often, to the point of tearful laughability, there is the assumption that only through a sameness that supervenes along vectors of identity that are deemed most important can we develop a sense of ethical relation. Subtending all of this, it seems to me, is a frustrating insistence that *because* one is ostensibly the same on the grounds of race or, for the more specific purposes of this meditation, gender, as others, *then* (note the causational logic) we can be in ethical relation. If you were not this thing, you'd be asked to leave. And for so long I have thought and felt, understanding quite intimately the whys and wherefores of these presumptions, how sad that we could not make kin and comrades on other, sometimes wildly other, grounds.

The concern is an ethical one. It is a concern for how we are permitted or not permitted to share life with others. To require doing this only through vectors of specific criteria—gender, for example, which is always shot through a logic of cisness and gender alignment and normative gendered enactment—is to then disallow a more ethical relation. *What if*, Denise Ferreira da Silva asks, *ethical descriptions had at their core a commonality that is not mediated by identity (as a shared particularity that is familial, national, historical)?* This formulation, the formulation of the "What if?" is so intriguing. It immediately launches us into the realm of the imagination. "What if?" is asking us to imagine, right now, another kind of arrangement. In short, the "What if?" is perhaps the sound of the keys dangling, or the lockpicking, or the window shattering, or the fence being jumped, all of which portend a jailbreak of these regimes of gender, of racialization. *What if ethical descriptors did not presume substantive or formal commonality (identity or equality)?*[*] The floodgates would open.

Let us put it more directly for our purposes: What if we did not and could not—the latter here, of course, the case, I would argue—presume that we were on equal ethical footing simply because we're all women here, we're all queer here, that is, equal ethical footing equalized by way of the unequal ethical footing presumed in being a woman in relation to a man or queer to straight? (Not to mention the myriad other

---

[*]Denise Ferreira da Silva

combinations that exceed such binaries and sexuality-focused queerness.) It is because the identificatory is not innocent nor a transparent ground on which we can then assume a trajectory of much more substantive things—inviting an understanding of nonbinary as *not an identity*, but rather the refusal of the criteria needed to live up to the identities we are forced to have. To purportedly be a thing says little of a subject and how that subject moves in relation to me and others; what more, indeed, do I know of you if I "know" that you "are" a woman? What do I know about how you will respond when I tell you this or that, when you encounter this idea or that person, when you are called on to do a certain kind of work? Precisely nothing.

Maybe this is why I found odd needing to hang out with the "boys" growing up. And even then, as I do now, I wondered why, what is it about one's ostensible gender that causally links them to others of that supposed gender? What are the things about that gender that destine one to a trajectory compatible with others of that ostensible gender, and what happens if one rejects that destiny? (Though of course they cannot—it's destiny. [So why all the policing and making sure that I fall in line? Why the constant attempts to wrangle strayers if this is, indeed, just the way things are?]) For so, so long I've wanted very little to do with this.

And it may be because the kind of (non)subject I've long wanted to become could not abide the categorical delimitations that then mandated strict forms of relationality. I did not want that, and I imagine few others want that, though those others do indeed exist. So the question then was, as it is now, more forcefully and precisely, on what else might one forge coalition? Or, further still, what happens to coalitional impulses—how are they tweaked and tinkered with, how are they made more robust, how differently do they feel—when the glue, as it were, is not one's same or similar identity, one's same or similar race or gender, one's approximation of a mythical, hegemonic norm but rather to where one is heading, what rhythmic groove one treads along, when they break free? Or even still, when they've become via having been being free? When they reject the community and its mutedly tiring undercurrents: that of wholeness and sameness and assimilation; that of cohesion and automatic safety; that of mutual interests; that of disciplining and shaping. If I, and many others, my (un)gender radical goons, do not wish to predicate our relationality, the very possibility of our relationality, on an adherence to notions of gender—to be a part of the supposed community we are told to ascribe to—that might mean we offer some other way to inaugurate being and becoming with others. Such ways might prove more expansive and open and consensual, such ways might prove more robust and radical and loving. Do we not owe ourselves, at least, that?

So much of what it seems community means is the pedestaling of a sameness assumed to promote safety, a sameness assumed to lead, indeed, to a pervasive sameness: same likes, same politics, same place or origin, same orientation to life. And that has not been true. Identificatory signifiers become impenetrably metonymic, which is to say they become the foreclosure of thinking, of generatively suspending, of inquiring, of curiosity. To put forth the identificatory as metonymic of other robust modalities of sociality disallows thought and modalities of life that do not adhere to the strictures embedded in ultimately normative parameters of life's and sociality's scope. If the identificatory relies, at base, on a violent *binarism*—you are inside or outside, you are this or that, you come to this space by the approved means or you have no place in this space—then that which one moves through when they desire relationality and coalition on no grounds, via unsanctioned means and means that opt out of the very logics orchestrating relationality, is the nonbinaristic—not some tepid "gender nonbinariness" but the philosophical, critical, asubjective modality of engendering another mode of existence not predicated on the logics of exclusion nor the logics, even, of inclusion. Let's say someone like Foucault, that sexually radical philosopher and historian, would understand this as what he terms a "way of life." It would then mean that nonbinariness *is not to identify with the psychological traits and the visible masks of the homosexual,* or the "androgynous" or "genderqueer" or what have you, and it is because the nonbinary, not an identity or gender proper, *can be shared among individuals of different age, status, and social activity. It can yield intense relations not resembling those that are institutionalized. It seems to me that a way of life can yield a culture and an ethics.*[†] Were my friendships so long ago friendships attempting to way-of-life, as verb, nonbinary tethers to others?

I think so, and I want this to be so. I want us to come together in friendship not because we both identify as nonbinary. Again, we are not talking about how you or I identify, for this is so fraught with claiming labels we didn't need to create in the first place, too fraught with ending at the saying of oneself as this thing without much consideration for the vast tidal wave of what else constitutes life and living. What we are talking about, I want to say as kindly as I can, is coming together in friendship because we both are attempting to emerge onto a plane of existence through a discarding of gender's clutches. To *be* nonbinary is more like believing in nonbinary: believing that this world's strict twoness is nowhere near enough, that we can love each other and cultivate fields for ourselves and one another by letting us, irrespective of what gender has said we need to be, learn of one another, un-preempted by gender's presumptuousness. Nonbinariness invites us to gather together, where such a gathering is to *believe in (but not look for) its unseen/unfracked depths of undisclosed place and activity, unindicated space-times of interspecies relation.* Here, we do not come together because we already have one another figured out, locked into often binaristic systems that dictate how we are even allowed to show up—an allowance very much predicated on being properly this gender *or* that gender, no in-between, no declining to state—but we come together without needing to need gender, that behemoth of burying ourselves and who we could be with each other. Here,

---

[†]Michel Foucault

in this gathering, this *figural in-betweenness, moving between rescaled relations among*‡ anything and everything, we do not play by the rules of gender; we play other games, patty-caking without shackled hands and jump-roping without chained ankles. When we play without needing to confirm or check or validate or verify or discipline proper manners of speech or hands or legs or proximities or behaviors. Nonbinary life, inextricable from which is nonbinary friendship—our NBFFs, our homenbies—engages the *experiment of material, elemental, and unframeable communion, a togetherness ungiven to art's,* or this life's, *own formal rendering, moving as possible and impossible sociality.* We need not do or be what they've said; there is more, so much more, to experiment with.

Get this: I was gifted the opportunity to spend a week in Berlin with a group of amazing thinkers. Many of them were from Argentina, their particular lilt of Spanish a joy to listen to. And nearly all of them were folks who think deeply about gender. One of the people there was my friend and supporter from afar and at times up close, Susan Stryker. Susan—if I may, and I think I know I may—is one of the most gracious and intellectually, socially astute entities walking this planet right now. We communed, in a real sense; we shared and thought and laughed; she taught me, all of us, so much. She and I walked the long trek from a museum back to our lodging, talking about a miraculous range of things—she even invited to introduce me to Sandy Stone. I learned so much about her, and she learned more about me. In that week, conversing with Susan and so many others, I experienced the achievement, temporary as it may have been, of a perpetual *questing for noncoercive communion.*§

---

‡Sarah Jane Cervenak
§Ashon Crawley

On the Thursday of that week, I and the rest of the group traveled into downtown Berlin where Susan and two other trans elders would be discussing contemporary trans life. It was exquisite; it was an honor. Afterward, all in attendance scampered up to the rooftop—as one does on summer evenings in Europe—and I waited in line for a bottle of water and some assorted cheeses (also as one does in Europe). A tap on the shoulder.

"Are you Marquis Bey?" the person behind me asks. "I am, yes," I respond, just shy of completely confused. "Oh my god, so sorry to bother you, but I love your work. How are you doing?"

Let me set the stage a little bit more: This is only my second time outside of the country in which I was born. I am in Berlin, where I have never been before, at an event where I know no one but the folks I came with, almost all of whom have also never been to Berlin before. Now, someone—who, as you'll learn shortly, is also not from Berlin—recognizes me and alludes to having encountered my writing. All at this event that I was a mere spectator at.

The person, who turned out to be astonishingly lovely, was named Emma. She happened to be in Berlin, leaving in the next couple days, and stumbled upon this trans event (now, as one does when one is in Europe and is trans). Emma is French and a philosopher and a dancer and gearing up to co-parent a child on a commune with a bunch of other trans folks. Emma, in short, is marvelous. We talk for over three hours, the conversation ending only because it is past midnight and the venue is closing and I most definitely need someone I came with to show me how to use the subway to get back to where we were staying. But that conversation with Emma will, and has continued to, live with me—it was a deeply, unapologetically trans conversation where gender was toyed with, discarded, insulted, left in the corner never to be thought about again. It was a conversation where I did not feel like I had to do gender at all; a conversation, it was, where gender did not have to orchestrate in formulaic scriptural ritual how we ought to weave our existential moments on a summer Thursday in Berlin into one another. Gender's refusal, our conversational coalitional nonbinariness, permitted an unlikely friendship. What a gift: that encounter was infinitesimally unlikely, next to impossible. And it happened, because that is what this gift, this nonbinaristically trans gift, is: the giving of the khôra, that which precedes and exceeds the structures of modernity—namely, here, the ways gender structures everything, tyrannically—and it is *impossible. Not impossible but the impossible.*[1]

Emma kept in touch, asked for a favor that I gladly agreed to, and later sent me a note. Even after more than a year, after the impossibility of our meeting, Emma leapt to me. What Emma said I will never forget. Upon reflecting on that encounter, Emma writes that it was *the profound gift of nonbinariness as a pastpresentfuture of trans: refusing the grounds onto which we have been said so far.* And that sent me somewhere. There are grounds we are said to stand on, and those grounds are what determine what we can be, who we can be, who we can meet and love and know. We are said, determined, thrown into a very particular kind of existence because of these grounds. This is what the ground permits and says, so it must be so. Except nonbinariness, that pastpresentfuture of trans, its evil triplet, need not adhere to these grounds. Nonbinariness ungrounds and says nothing of us. We emerge, floating, unsaid because what is there to say? Only what can move through us, not needing to say anything at all.

What a beautiful way to think about friendship. We come together and stay together not because it is said, predetermined before we arrive, our communion prearranged by those who don't even know us, but because there are no criteria that preexist us, no requisites we need to heed in order to truly engage, no automatic foreclosures to our bond or mechanisms that dictate the permissible parameters of how we can be together. There are those who, I know, might say that their

---

[1] Jacques Derrida

friendships have been possible and have grown unshakable *because* of gender—these are my *girls*, they might say; or, my *boys* are my ride or dies. Yes, and that is wonderful. But I do not believe that it is because of their ascription to gender that they have forged such a bond. Those girls might know why you're crying before even you know (as old-school Destiny's Child has taught us) or those boys might have been next to you when you lived through a trauma. And we need these people. I simply don't want us to think that gender was the reason why we were able to survive it when in many cases gender might have been exactly the culprit that imperiled us in the first place. We must wonder: is the ongoingness of such friendships truly because of gender, or might it have been the vector through which we were disciplined into allowing ourselves to interact with certain kinds of people in certain kinds of ways? For some, the invocation of gender in friendships—*my girls*; *my boys*, the perpetual prepubescence notwithstanding—can function as a survival strategy. It can signify loyalty forged through shared struggle, often too painful to articulate: These are the people who held me through the darkest nights, when words didn't suffice. Perhaps the ability to connect was entered via gender; perhaps we were in proximity to one another, invited or forced to be intimate with one another through gender— through these scripted playdates that we just kept having as we got older, or this sex-segregated basketball league—but gender, I think, didn't make the bond strong. It was something else, something wider and more vast and more capacious than gender could ever hope to be.

Maybe I just want, unrealistically, a different way to be friends. And maybe I've been doing that all along. I want NBFFs, friends who need not "be" nonbinary—though by now I hope we know that the NB is not some kind of corporeally composed requisite—but who know how to do relationality a bit differently. Those with whom we are friends because we know something about not heeding grammars of coming together in proper ways. We know that when we converse, we need not follow the codes and scripts; when we sit and break bread, we know we need not behave in this or that way. How often have we seen mom and dad talk only of logistics and the weather, or brother-in-law "Yes, ma'am" his girlfriend and swoop in to "protect" her from a harsh word yet have little interest in her otherwise? How often has a binary understanding of and concession to gender, concession to gender as such, meant that we don't talk, don't learn, don't know, don't actually care, don't listen, don't fucking love one another at all, only the fantasmatic bloodbath that has become the only image of another we can see? We've deemed endemic discrimination by way of gender some kind of insight into someone, without recognizing that *the very existence of gender allows for discrimination based on gender*, demands discrimination, violation, as the means by which gender is done. Might we all *benefit from the deconstruction of gender if first we are brave enough to conceive of it?*[#]

I say all this, and yet my circle is somewhat small. There aren't throngs of people in my contacts whom I reach out to everyday. There isn't a best friend who I've known since kindergarten who has been my Day 1. There is, in fact, quite a lot of silence, numerous lulls, even more "I owe you a text"s. And you know what? That is okay. These friendships are not anxious, needing to be affirmed and reaffirmed constantly.

Like Danny. Danny, we've known each other since January 2011. Your nonbinariness and mine are different yet so woven together. It is video games and philosophy, our respective nonbinaries; it is taking ideas and thoughts and politics, as my dear mentor C. Riley Snorton has told me, as deeply and as seriously as they'll allow. We do that together, you and me. And we will continue doing that, interspersed with which *Final Fantasy* game I should start with, memes about how we forgot to respond to a text not because we don't care but because "darkness took me. And I strayed out of thought and time. Stars wheeled overhead and every day was as long as the life age of the earth. But I'm good now, how are you?"

[#]LJ

You texted me on February 25, 2024, the year in which I am writing this. You were voicing frustrations, compounded by the death of Nex Benedict. And this is what you, vulnerably, graciously, trustingly said:

Saying this here, because I don't know who else to say it to that would hear it for what it is, and my thoughts on the matter are unfinished and angry (and thus vulnerable to those who would not treat them generously):

Nex Benedict. A non-binary, Choctaw (but "white-passing") kid, who was growing up in Oklahoma. Was. Because beat senseless by women in a bathroom in the wake of a recently passed anti-trans state law that forces people to use the bathroom of their assigned gender at birth. Now dead. Dead because of that.

When M— [one of Danny's partners, redacted here for privacy] saw the news about Nex, they did a double take and asked if we were related because, in many features, we look a lot alike. It's startling in some ways, especially those deep, dark eyes.

Me, then. A non-binary, Choctaw (but at first glance "white-passing") kid, who almost grew up in Oklahoma. I haven't been beaten, or to death.

Yet, on top of the casual "oops I just assume you are a white man" (then continues to assume so) that is nearly an everyday experience, which I ignore with my usual grace, I have had my trans-ness and indigeneity challenged and/or outright denied in sometimes deeply ruthless and malicious ways.

I get it … I look how I look, and it is /easy/ to manipulate optics. Historical nondigenous erasure has been so successful that good liberal people don't even feel bad about denying it whether out of "good intentions" or opportunistically, as if that isn't still yet another instance of the erasure they sometimes express "solidarity" with confronting. And sure,

I don't perform androgyny or go out of my way to make my non-binary-ness perform to people's expectations. [And you need not do this, friend. We owe them nothing; to try to conform to a fabricated image of nonbinariness only confirms cisnormativity's illogic that to look a certain way calculated by cisnormativity is the only valid way to "be" that thing. Fuck that.] *I don't have the energy. Sure, it's a choice in some ways. I'm not trying to complain, either— so very many have suffered even greater things. I get it. I endure.*

But the real killer? The most malicious and ruthless manipulations have been delivered at the hands of people fully invested in DEIA discourse, who have, it seems, learned to use it as a source of personal advancement and power. It is easy to crucify or kill a white-passing Choctaw masc- (or fem-) presenting non-binary person when it suits a (liberal) need. And it is easy to raise their flag when it suits a (liberal) need, too.

Suffice it therefore to say that it is killing me a little to see some of them at whose hands I have suffered in these ways plaster Nex Benedict's face all over insta reels and calls for justice. It is stirring up all kinds of consulted feelings and conflicting thoughts, like a Gordian knot. Because what can I even say about it?

And I'm not saying anything new, I know. It's all been said before. Great thoughts, Daniel.

And they were and are great thoughts, Danny. (You know you have never been Daniel to me, always Danny.) You are voicing an affective depth springing from, I think, a yearning for a pervasive nonbinariness. They praise the slain nonbinary kid as a way to bolster their own justice bona fides, yet when it comes to you, another nonbinary kid who does not fit the bill as neatly for their liberalism, such compassion is not there. You are not saying that you are Nex Benedict, but you are saying that you are strikingly, eerily close in many ways, making the disconnect between those who have raised Nex's banner while sullying yours all the more stark. You are not saying the two of you are the same, but you are saying that you, too, could be beaten just the same.

I loved the text. It showed me that we have something quite deep and transtemporal, transspatial—needing not to be in the same place or the same timeline—thinking and living alongside and by way of one another. I hearted it, of course, and responded as lovingly and with as much gratitude as I could. Because that you could share this, yourself, with me, in such a moment as this, that was friendship. That was love. I wonder how many others who have lived and died have been able to feel that kind of love.

*I hadn't heard about this person and this murder, so I appreciate you bringing it to my attention. And it must feel deeply unsettling in a lot of ways—the similarities between the two of you, the felt proximity to a murderous fate. I feel that *for* you, though of course I can't really do that. I suppose what I mean is that I feel the possibility of a deep part of me, wrapped up in you and in us, being expunged so swiftly, so casually. And then the DEI whoever-the-fucks using that as a way to brand and propound their lukewarm liberal politics ("Look at me on the right side of history because I'm 'mourning' the loss of a queer person. It's about me, actually"). Those people are probably the most frustrating—purportedly well meaning, but sutured to really troubling ways of thinking, and very mainstream, deeply non-radical ways of thinking, foreclosing the kind of world and politics we are striving toward. And nonbinariness seems to be a really potent testing ground, so to speak, to see where are you really at, person who is supposedly down for the cause. All this is to say I feel alongside you, in different but deeply felt ways.*

And of course the day after sending this text, I heard so much about Nex Benedict. I felt, all over again, sad and afraid for you. I wanted, and continue to want, to protect you. You are not the biggest person, and I know others might, and perhaps have, used that against you, trying to physically intimidate you. But know that Marquis is still from Philly, and Philly has taught me about something: it is not a violence that runs through me as if demarcating a territory not to be invaded; it is knowing that vulnerability betides us all in variegated ways, and when others unsheathe their vulnerabilities upon some, I do not wish to let that go uninterrupted. That others lament how they've been disallowed power or status, or have been harmed, they sometimes propound that violence onto others as a way to find stability in a world that secures us based on who we can position ourselves over or above. There are people who have been financially harmed, physically harmed, emotionally harmed, and who are vulnerable more than others in these ways—and these vulnerabilities sometimes do and sometimes don't supervene along racialized and gendered lines. It is another thing how the things we've been made vulnerable to are weaponized, how we respond to how we are positioned and feel in ways that intensify others' vulnerabilities and harms. And that is so often where you fall prey: you and I know intimately, if that 1:00 a.m. call all those years ago is indicative of anything, that you are so often physically, sexually vulnerable, and others have tried to hurt you, have hurt you. So with you, Danny, I mean this: *Someone starts problems out here, you call me. / That's my business*,** because I'm not about to let anyone erase who I know is one of the biggest possibilities for the future of my, of our, nonbinary life.

Or Esbi, *mi chuleta*, always with the quick wit and blunt—though incisive—critiques of The Straights™. We began, from day, like, six, forging life together through a certain refrain from doing gender in the ways we've both been told. You loved me in ways not beholden to that from which the nonbinary departs. There were bumps, absolutely, misnames and misgenders and

---

**Joshua Bennett

the creeping invasion of the cisnormative that tried entering. But with you, together, we were always, always able to hold what we had and have in such elastic strength.

It started when we first connected, and you told G-man—your mother, my mother-in-law, bless her—that you met this lovely person who is nonbinary, and how that means they do not identify (a word we both shy away from now) as a man or a woman, that they use they pronouns. That was me, is me. Even then, you were holding me. And it started again when I read to you some thoughts I had, about how I am not and do not wish to be a man, how that then screws up sexuality because the very notion of sexuality is predicated on gender being a thing, so if gender is not a thing for me—and now, for us—what could "sexuality" possibly mean for us? And then it started, once more—all these beginnings, all these starts and returns—when you shared with me that you wanted another name, and you wanted, not another gender but *no gender*. In that moment, in our bed, the morning sun shining in from the skylights, you opened yourself more to and with me, inviting me into another way to love you.

And, in fact, it started yet again when we were expressing our frustrations with you-know-who, the one who was thrown into our lives and who we were forced to endure. She, we said, did white-girl-ness; from the self-infantilized voice to the not knowing you aren't supposed to get out of the car when you get pulled over (and the absolutely stentorian silence we had when she said "I was going to cry, 'cause I heard some people [which people, huh?] do that, but I didn't wanna give him the satisfaction") to the messing up both of our pronouns (mine more than yours, and we of course speculated as to why the disparity) to the damsel in distress I need protection from my big strong boyfriend and am intimidated when Marquis asks me basic questions about what I think and the glaring problematics of those (lack of) thoughts. We do not care that or if she "is" a white girl—that very particular brand of gendered personhood with the longest history of violence that is often not called violence. No, what we care about, and what we bristle at, is how she propounds that gendered personhood, slips into it like a birthright, and is oblivious to how she slips and slips and slips so effortlessly.

We talked about this on and off one day, and another day, and any other days when she Kool-Aid Man'd into the walls of our serenity, and one of the more profound things I recall us discussing is how we, not to venerate ourselves, do not have to do such things. Because we do not have to do gender. See, she—let's call her, I don't know, Q or something … See, Q or something desires gender *so* much; she needs gender in order to talk to us, to talk to her boyfriend, to talk about the boring and hella troubling things she's learning or talking about in school. She brings gender to our home and buckles when we try to sweep it off our porch. And maybe that is in part why she is so jarring: we have orchestrated our living and loving together through other modes of care and love that do not think of gender's presence, and then here she comes. We, as we discussed, do not have to ascribe gender to this way that we ought to fold into one another or that behavioral idiosyncrasy. We, in short, are free. We are free of having to play the games, perform the roles, limit ourselves to this track.

Or maybe all this was too overlong, and I could have just rehashed the joke that we use to characterize to others the trajectory of our relationship: What does a lesbian bring to a second date? A U-Haul—because we planned an eight-day road trip together after only two weeks of knowing one another; we moved in together after a month and a half. Even then, *lesbian* did not merely mean woman who was romantic with other women. That language describes neither of us. Lesbian, even then, for us had the inflection given to us by that French philosophical gender abolitionist; *"woman" has meaning only in heterosexual systems of thought and heterosexual economic systems.* "Lesbian" is not a woman, but the designation for the kind of person who has said that gender shall no longer circumscribe how I love, how I think, or how I am with myself and others. Lesbian for us then and certainly now is one who seeks through their inhabitation of the world off-kilter to *destroy politically, philosophically, and symbolically the categories of "men" and "women."*[††] Lesbians indeed are not women, they—we, as the joke implied for us— gift nonbinary life.[1]

*
**

NBFFs are not, simply put, friends who are nonbinary. They are so, so much more than this. They are open questions allowing me to inquire about them and myself and, too, what we might imagine as another kind of life. 'Cause I don't want or need to be friends with someone who has themselves all figured out, impenetrable to anything else, rigid and fixed and in lockstep with the criteria laid out by that which they know themselves to be. Because then, how do we swirl through one another? How could we even begin to existentially curl through conversations where we don't have much figured out but have questions and curiosities? If you've finished yourself, all coherent and locked in, there is no more room for other things, no room for the horizon where what is on the other side might, hopefully, be nothing like what could have been expected. This questioning is reserved for no specific demographic. Those who have figured it all out span the gamut; Esbi's The Straights are surely like this, but so too are the transgenders and the queers and nonbinary identitarians. And we don't really have much for all of them right now. Again, NBFFs are not just nonbinary or transgender or queer friends; that is not enough. NBFFs are those, at least for now, who keep wondering.

[††]Monique Wittig

Epilogue

To write of nonbinary life is neither easy nor simple. But it is work that needs to be done. This work—at once discursive, political, coalitional, singular, imaginative, and so many other things—has been, here in this treatise, a joy, at the same time it has been an intellectually and socio-politically challenging endeavor. But that is the work, and it must be chosen every time.

We live in a world that insists on legibility, categorization, and the relentless enforcement of gender. From the mundane to the spectacular, gender is imposed; from the job application and video game character creation screen to the enforcement of gender through assault and invasive psychological assessment. Gender swirls around us without end, it seems, but here we try to cease the swirling. That is nonbinary life. *Nonbinary Life* has attempted to write toward the release of gender—a loosening of its grip in the name of letting it drift into irrelevance rather than trying to replace it. A world where the signposts of he and she fade not into another option but into an open field, where being is not confined by grammar's need to categorize before it can let one arrive to the encounter.

This book has been a collection of stories, reflections, and theoretical musings, all orbiting around the central question: What does it mean to live a life that refuses gender? It is a question that cannot be answered definitively, for the definitive is yet another gesture of taxonomization that nonbinary, in its elusive non-categoricality, (un)marks a dissent from. But that life is one that seeks to exist, fully exist, in the crevices of a system that would rather see us neatly categorized and contained for the purposes of surveillance, for the maintenance of the status quo, for the ease of those who wish to enforce gender as a stable referent in service of disciplining, circumscribing, rather than recognizing it as an arbitrary imposition.

But let us be clear: nonbinary life is paltry and uninteresting if it is only not-man, not-woman; that is, if nonbinary life is only an echo of the binary, a shadow cast by its terms rather than a world unmoored from them. I wonder what kind of "life" that is, one that merely negates without overflowing into other possible modes of being. What, then, fills that chasm with something else, something unanticipated, something that cannot be captured by existing logics? Do not let them say to you, incorrectly and misguidedly, that nonbinary is "just" rejecting gender for some faddish reason, as if what we are suggesting is simply and straightforwardly the opposite of the binary, or a third category to be slotted into the existing framework. Nonbinary life is a refusal of the logic that underpins gender, a gesture of fixity and categorization, itself. It is a refusal to accept that gender is inevitable, natural, or necessary. And when it is not inevitable, think of the pantheon of relations, embodiments, and unfixed intimacies that we can now move through, be held by, revel in. Indeed, live and feel that pantheon.

To say nonbinariness is a *life* is to affirm its weight—it is not merely an identity among others or a footnote to transness. It is a critical insistence that the category of gender itself is suspect. Nonbinary life as we've thought through it here asserts that nonbinariness is not just a refusal of man or woman, but a dismantling of the grammar that makes those positions intelligible, a dismantling of gender *as such*. It aims at the unworking of gender as a schema that has long been tethered to regimes of legibility, violence, and governance. Nonbinary life is thus not an identity to be respected but a politics to be pursued—a politics that seeks to abolish the conditions under which "gender" becomes necessary, desirable, here in any capacity.

It is not going to be a smooth ride, though. Many of us know this already, all the challenging and saddening—perhaps even hostile and violent—conversations and interactions we've had to have a testament to the difficulty of truly, unapologetically, genuinely living nonbinary life. The accusations of delusion, the insistence that gender is biology, the medicalized gaze that seeks to recontain us in the language of sexed bodies, as if to say: come back to the real, return to the known. Biology is only real inasmuch as we have agreed upon its meaning, its edges, its significance, what counts and when, how we draw the lines and what we call statistically significant. To insist on the primacy of "biological sex" is to tether oneself to the epistemological framework that nonbinary life refuses—a framework that craves the stability of a referent, the fixity of a foundation. Perhaps what we call biological sex is already subsumed within the regulatory fictions of gender itself. As Susan Stryker has written, *this so-called "sex of the body" is an interpretive fiction that narrates a complex amalgamation of gland secretions and reproductive organs, chromosomes and genes, morphological characteristics, and physiognomic features. There are far more than two viable aggregations of sexed bodily being,* and far more important things that impact how we inhabit the world, how we interact, what we desire and know and feel, who we wish to be with, engage, and encounter, how we love and don't love and yearn. What does "biology," really, do for us? To "know" one's "biology" does what now, exactly? To invoke "biological sex," then, is not to reintroduce a materialist corrective but to reassert a carceral grammar of classification. Nonbinary life demands otherwise: not a reconciliation with sexed intelligibility but a refusal of its claim altogether. For *We never*—and I mean that, never—*experience or know ourselves as a body pure and simple, i.e. as our "sex."*[*] As a category, biology demands recognition because its

---

*Judith Butler

coherence relies on a disciplinary structure that punishes those who dare to ask: must it be this way?

What rests on the other side of this is something that cannot swat away the biological, or the binaristic, and assumes that all things deemed "nonbinary" will be easy and clean. There is mess on the other side. But what a mess it is, a mess that needs not be cleaned or denigrated. A mess worth living amid. *Nonbinary Life*, I hope, has not been a utopian vision. It is not a fantasy of a world without struggle or conflict. More than that, it invites a demand that we rethink the foundations of how we understand ourselves and each other. This demand is in light of the systems of power that rely on gender to maintain control, the institutions that enforce gender through violence and coercion, the people who perpetuate gender through their words and actions and, perhaps most importantly, the ways we, too, have internalized and reproduced the logics of gender, the ways we have disciplined ourselves and others into recognizability. The refusal of gender is not only an external confrontation; it is an internal reckoning as well.

This is not a call to clarity or legibility, nor a plea for inclusion under the current terms. I am arguing, quite specifically, for a life that does not rely on recognition from the structures that gender us. Nonbinariness, in this sense, is not just oppositional but abolitionist. It asks us not to build better cages for ourselves but to destroy the cage. In this sense nonbinary is and must be aligned with other refusals—with black radical refusals, queer fugitive practices, anti-carceral demands—that imagine the possibility of living beyond what this world permits.

Nonbinary life cannot simply be the everyday goings-on of people who identify as nonbinary. It is for anyone who has felt, even in fleeting moments, that gender is not enough. That gender is too constraining. That gender has demanded of them something they could never truly be. It is for those who have questioned, who have whispered to themselves in the quiet of their own minds: why this? Why this, and not something else? It is for those who know, somewhere in the abyss and untamed, that something else is possible.

This is the world we are fighting for. This is the world we are building. And this is the world we will create, together.

Toward the otherwise of gender, the otherwise of us,

—Marquis

NOTES

"Gender Is Not the Thing"

1 Thank you, Elyx, for this incredible, deep conversation.

2 An incisive retort courtesy of my friend and colleague, Nick Winters. He is referencing without citation, incisively so, the ways that even the feminist among us, even the trans among us, the radical, they, too, sometimes are willfully acting, as SA Smythe writes in "Black Life, Trans Study," "as … 'non-sworn cops,' in this instance, of the colonial gender binary."

3 We simply cannot suggest that whiteness entails a universally unproblematic relationship to gender or that gender has been uniformly "given" to all white people. Rather, it points to the ways whiteness and colonial modernity construct and enforce gender as a racialized hierarchy. Both the deprivation or enforcement of gender—because that's what it is for white folks in this framework, not a giving but an enforcement, a threat, as it were—operates as a mechanism of white supremacy, thus we must complicate any simplistic ethical imperative to preserve gender.

4 Why? Because I want to always, as much as possible, hold out hope for the possibility that the tall person never even knew that there were other ways to be. So in not gendering the tall person, we gift this person a new experience: not having to think of oneself as gendered, which might be the beginning, possibly, of coming to a new way of understanding oneself as not having to be gendered. Because no one ever told you that was okay for you. So here we are, saying that is okay. Run with it if you'd like.

Burner Gender

1   Grandma does this. Grandma is getting older—seventy-five now—and she is starting to, humorously, not yet worryingly, misname us. Perhaps she wants to get the attention of my sister, Tianna. "Toya," she would say, my mother's name. Then, "I mean Gordon," my brother. "Junior," my uncle—may he rest in peace. "Marquis," me, who hasn't lived there in fifteen years. Then finally my sister's name. We laugh at her, and she is good-spirited, chuckling too. "Oh, you know who I'm talking to." And we do. To be called a wrong name does not disqualify your name, does not mean you did not know who was being called even though it was not your name.

2   And we can't forget too that in this, "Arya" wouldn't even be the name we use for this entity. "Arya" also goes.

3   Okay, so androgyny is, in its simplest lay definition, to be both masculine and feminine, or to be unidentifiably man or woman—to at once be andro (man) and gyno (woman), right? Nuances will bubble up for some, I'm sure, but let's just go with this. Who has decided that X kind of presentation is decidedly masculine, and Y is feminine? How are you so sure that this *is* masculine and feminine, in equal measure (or unequal; the quantities don't matter)? My point is that what has counted or qualified as masculine or feminine has undergone so much variation, and is contemporarily fractured along geographical, cultural, and racial lines that "being androgynous" does not mean something as obvious as one might think. It is only obvious if one has a very particular notion of masculinity and femininity, which, to me, is kinda the point of what I'm saying: that gender, the handmaidens for which are masculinity and femininity, and a whole host of others, is to be thrown into excruciating crisis and done away with. How, then, can masculinity or femininity retain any meaning, let alone value? This is not a critique of how you personally *ought* to express yourself sartorially or corporeally, only to query skeptically the process of ascribing those to gendered camps that you deem you are blending, as if the meaning of those two camps is not also, perpetually, incessantly, under crisis and unable to maintain stability.

4 I do not "identify" as nonbinary—or anything, really—because
identity and identification are insufficient substitutes for relation
and disposition, desire, enactment, and engagement. Identification
presumes a static relation to selfhood, a kind of anchoring
I fundamentally resist. To say I "identify" as nonbinary is to
suggest I've located myself within a ready-made category, a box
now labeled more accurately than the previous one. "Identifying"
makes it seem like I've chosen a side, picked a flag, declared
an allegiance, when what I am doing is much messier, more
fleeting, more unbeholden. I do not identify as nonbinary so
much as I move nonbinarily, live nonbinarily, think and agitate
nonbinarily, ache and unmake in ways that trouble the call to
name at all. What matters to me is not the solidity of the term but
the refusal it carries—refusal of legibility, of finality, of capture.

The Evil Triplet

1 The term community feels more like an imagined collective
predicated on a certain kind of sameness—you belong here, but
there are certain kinds of entities that don't belong here—or an
imposition of similarity and staticness that may very well not
be the case. "Community" is too flat, rigid, and presumptuous
for me. It marks a totalizing knowledge over what is inside
the supposed community, and this interior is maintained by
distinguishing itself from an, often threatening, exterior. This
notion of the interior, the community, is not to be trusted, is
not serving the radical aims we aspire toward. Nevada writes
in *The Abolition of Law* that the "racial," and I would also say
the "gendered," is a form of attempted ontological community,
capturing and disallowing exiting of those forced (yes, forced)
to "belong," *a priori*, to that community. But community, which
is to say the racial, the gendered, the categorical, *is nothing
more than the inherited legacy of police control, dressed up in
varying degrees of progressive discourse*, says Nevada. *For there
to be an outside, there must be an inside with borders in need of
protection. The investigation of who does and does not belong—
in a neighborhood or in a riot—has at its heart the desire for the
fort, which cannot lead us to any meaningful form of abolition. It*

is the fort that must be abolished too. The fort is the ontological, the supposed community that comes with being a part of the same race or gender or what have you. Nonbinary has no interest in the fort either, even if—or when—the fort is all we are said to have.

2   There are many other vectors through which one might gain desire and arousal that are not predicated on gender, or that radically revise gender. In other words, sexuality need not be located solely or primarily in gendered inflection points. One could very well feel desire for a nonhuman entity, for objects, for ways of thinking and speaking, for a number of sexual partners (who need not all have the same gender or gender at all; who need not all be the same species) or frequency of sexual acts or kind of sexual acts; these sexual acts need not even involve genitals.

3   See my essay "On Lived Experience," as well as Joan W. Scott's "The Evidence of Experience." I say: "In short, simply because we have been accosted by oppressions of various sorts does not make us exorbitantly wise. We do not become experts on the totality of oppressive systems if we happen to be affected by those systems. There must be more. The 'more' supplements, or lovingly critiques, the pervasive habit of 'plac[ing] importance on taking individuals' words at face value and honouring their expressed experience (that is, the lived experience they say they are having),' Kai Cheng Thom writes in the context of queer communities, because this practice 'seem[s] to be the norm in capital-C Community,' is 'reactive and unhelpful in a lot of situations.'" Scott writes: "To put it another way, the evidence of experience, whether conceived through a metaphor of visibility or in any other way that takes meaning as transparent, reproduces rather than contests given ideological systems—those that assume that the facts of history speak for themselves and, in the case of histories of gender, those that rest on notions of a natural or established opposition between sexual practices and social conventions"; "They take as self-evident the identities of those whose experience is being documented and thus naturalize their difference. They locate resistance outside its discursive construction, and reify agency as an inherent attribute of individuals, thus decontextualizing it. When experience is

taken as the origin of knowledge, the vision of the individual subject (the person who had the experience or the historian who recounts it) becomes the bedrock of evidence upon which explanation is built. Questions about the constructed nature of experience, about how subjects are constituted as different in the first place, about how one's vision is structured—about language (or discourse) and history—are left aside."

4   There are different camps of people out there, more than perhaps I even know. There are those who simply don't get it, don't agree, don't want to experience any semblance of acknowledging that one's pronouns could be anything other than what is "obvious." And we can challenge these people, insist on them using specific pronouns for us and others. I just wonder if that's the end of the fight. They use the "correct" pronoun now. Cool, now what? Do they think differently about gender? Does that pronoun for them come with a change in how they understand you? Because I am sure that many are, for example, like my brother-in-law, whom I love, who is shockingly good with pronouns but, in a heated exchange with him, revealed that he *still* sees me as a "male human." Getting it, pronouns, "right" does not then mean that the more important thing—the gendered and ungendered stuff of the person before you—is right too. It might even be the case that someone getting your pronouns correct implies to them that their job is done, that the pronoun *is* the entire job, when really it is only the beginning.

Or on the other hand, there are folks who do think shifting one's pronouns is "valid" (how I'm beginning to loathe this word) and who ultimately will use—or at least try—the pronouns you wish, but then also make whatever excuse to return to the comfort of he's and she's. Like, there was the episode of *Breaking Down Patriarchy* on Judith Butler, who uses they pronouns (at least at the time of writing), and after the host shares vulnerably and graciously that using they pronouns for someone is new to her and that she'd practice doing so in the episode, the guest, Maxine Hanks, responds that while she is comfortable using nonbinary gender pronouns she'll be using she for Butler because, and I quote, "It's cumbersome to use they/them pronouns in a conversation like this." (A conversation like what? How is using they pronouns cumbersome in a conversation on feminism and

the subversion of gender and the most influential gender theorist
of our contemporary moment? What is cumbersome about that?
Where the hell would these pronouns be non-cumbersome if not
in a conversation like this?) Anyway …

A ~~Man's~~ World

1 See note 8 of "Introduction: Abolition, Gender Radicality"
in *Black Trans Feminism*, and also *Cistem Failure: Essays on
Blackness and Cisgender*. There, and elsewhere, I've taken up
the question of my own identification—its tricky, seemingly
untenable, and often externally projected nature. People look at
me and see what they've been trained to see: "a 'black' 'man.' "
They read me through that frame. But what I insist on—what
I refuse to concede—is that these identifications are anything but
misrecognitions of and through a colonial schema. I am not a
man, not because I want another category, but because I reject
the system that demands one. And if I say I am not a man, many
nod or stumble; if I say I am not black (as race), panic starts
to creep in. I've never quite said that, and yet I gesture toward
its possibility, indeed its desired actualization. As I've argued in
"Incorporeal Blackness," another essay of mine, and throughout
my work, race, like gender, is an apparatus: hegemonic,
circumscribing, colonial. My refusals are refusals of the terms
themselves. That doesn't mean I float free of them, but that
I decline to participate in their authorization. People are often
unsure what to say of me. That's fine. I'm not looking for a name.
Ghosting these referents is not confusion—it is an intentional
practice of fugitivity. It is not absence, but an insistence on being
ungraspable, ungovernable, unrendered by the grammars of
capture.

2 Shared with permission. Thank you, MJ, for giving me permission
to share your words, and thank you for writing them.

NBFFs (Nonbinary Friends Forever)

1　I want to be clear too, as a way to keep a bit at bay the specter of appropriation or not taking lesbian life and its specificities seriously. Neither my partner nor I are "lesbians." We are not women, we "are" nonbinary; I was not assigned woman at birth, though this is not the case for my partner (notice also the negative construction of this second clause; there is nothing that it necessarily affirms). There are many who might say that such a joke or use of the term lesbian is inappropriate for me to use, and for myriad reasons. If this is you, I do apologize, sincerely, while also still maintaining that we ought to take Monique Wittig seriously: that lesbians are not women, are not any particular gender, which then means that it cannot be appropriated by another gender—lesbians have no gender to appropriate. My aim here, and I want to be as humble and honest and sincere about this as I can, is that the irreverence to gender that lesbian offers, and that my partner and I were picking up and running with, maps quite snugly onto us. If this is an offering of nonbinary life that does not obsess over adhering to criteria for validity as any specific gender and that yearns for expanding our possibilities for being outside of a hold over this or that gender to the exclusion of other kinds of gender, "lesbian" is perhaps Wittig's 1980s early iteration of a radical nonbinariness. It is in this spirit I offer these thoughts.

INDEX